Feminism, Community, and Communication

Feminism, Community, and Communication

Mary E. Olson
Guest Editor

Journal of Feminist Family Therapy
Volume 11, Number 4

Routledge
Taylor & Francis Group
New York   London

EDITOR

BETTY Mac KUNE-KARRER, MA
*Family Institute
Northwestern University
Evanston, IL 60201*

EDITOR ELECT

*Toni Schindler Zimmerman, PhD
Associate Professor
Department of Human Development
and Family Studies
Marriage and Family Therapy Program Director
Colorado State University
Fort Collins, CO 80523*

FOUNDING EDITOR

LOIS BRAVERMAN, ACSW
*3833 Woods Drive
Des Moines, IA 50312*

PAST EDITOR

JANINE ROBERTS, EdD
*University of Massachusetts
Amherst, MA*

ASSISTANT EDITOR

CATHERINE WEIGEL FOY, MSW
*The Family Institute
618 Library Place
Evanston, IL 60201*

ADVISING EDITOR

ELIZABETH A. CARTER, MSW
*Cagney Hill Road
Southfield, MA*

BOOK REVIEW EDITOR

ANNE C. BERNSTEIN, PhD
*The Wright Institute
2955 Shattuck Avenue
Berkeley, CA 94705*

MORRIS TAGGART, PhD
*8315 Braeside Lane
Houston, TX 77071-1227*

MOVIE/PLAY REVIEW EDITOR

JILL FREEDMAN, MSW
*636 Church Street, Suite 901
Evanston, IL 60201*

HUMOR EDITOR

THORANA NELSON, PhD
*Utah State University, FHD
College of Family Life
Department of Family & Human Development
Logan, UT 84322-2905*

RECRUITMENT EDITOR

MARY E. HOTVED, PhD
*1200 N. El Dorado Place
Tucson, AZ*

INTERVIEW EDITOR

CATHERINE WEIGEL FOY, MSW
*The Family Institute
618 Library Place
Evanston, IL 60201*

EDITORIAL BOARD

Constance R. Ahrons, PhD
*University of Southern California
Los Angeles, CA*
Judith Myers Avis, PhD
*University of Guelph
Department of Family Studies
Guelph, Ontario, Canada*
Claudia S. Bepko, ACSW
*Private Clinical Practice
Psychological Associates
Brunswick, ME*

Ellen M. Berman, MD
*321 Mallwyd Road
Merion, PA*
Michele Bograd, PhD
*Private Practice
Bedford, MA*
Pauline G. Boss, PhD
*University of Minnesota
St. Paul, MN*
Iris Cornelius, PhD
*The American Family Therapy Academy
Edina, MN*

Carrell Dammann, PhD
Open House, Inc.
Atlanta, GA

Judith Davis, EdD
University of Massachusetts
Amherst, MA

America Facundo, PhD
School of Medicine
Rio Piedras, PR

Celia J. Falicov, PhD
Private Practice

Nancy Boyd Franklin, PhD
Rutgers University
Graduate School of Applied
and Professional Psychology
New Brunswick, NJ

Adela G. Garcia, MA
Centro de Estudios Sistemicos
Buenos Aires, Argentina

Nydia Garcia-Preto, MSW
Family Institute of New Jersey
Metuchen, NJ

Virginia Goldner, PhD
Ackerman Institute for Family Therapy
New York, NY

Thelma Jean Goodrich, PhD
Columbia Presbyterian
Family Health Center
New York

Robert-Jay Green, PhD
California School
of Professional Psychology
Berkeley/Alameda

Beverly Greene, PhD
St. John's University
Brooklyn, NY

Mary Anna Ham, EdD
University of Massachusetts
Boston, MA

Rachel T. Hare-Mustin, PhD
Private Practice
Haverford, PA

Jennie Harré Hindmarsh, PhD, MSc, CQSW
Victoria University of Wellington
Wellington, New Zealand

Evan Imber-Black
Bronx Municipal Hospital Center,
Ackerman Institute for Family Therapy
New York, NY

Jennifer Iré, MPPM
University of Massachusetts
Amherst, MA

Jo-Ann Krestan, MA, CAC
Family Therapy Associates
Moab, UT

Molly Layton, PhD
Private Practice
Philadelphia, PA

Peliwe Lolwana, PhD
University of the Witwatersrand
Johannesburg, South Africa

William C. Madsen, PhD
Faculty, Family Institute of Cambridge
Cambridge, MA

Marilyn J. Mason
Private Practice
Adjunct Associate Professor
University of Minnesota
Minneapolis, MN

Monica McGoldrick, MSW
Director, Family Institute of New Jersey
Metuchen, NJ

Dusty Miller, EdD
Department of Clinical Psychology
Antioch University
Keene, NH

Marsha Pravder Mirkin, PhD
Private Practice
Newton, MA

Maria Blanca Moctezuma, PhD
Universidad de las Americas
Mexico, DF

Robert Pasick, PhD
Faculty, Ann Arbor Center
Ann Arbor, MI

Patricia Romney, PhD
64 Carriage Lane
Amherst, MA

Richard Schwartz, PhD
Associate Professor
University of Illinois at Chicago
Chicago, IL

Philippa Seligman, CQSW
Family Therapist, U.K.C.P. Registered
Wales, UK

Tazuko Shibusawa, PhD
Columbia University School
of Social Work
New York, NY

Olga Silverstein, MSW
Faculty Emeritus
Ackerman Institute for Family Therapy
New York, NY

Virginia Simons
Private Practice
Oberlin, OH

Kathy Stathos, LCSW
UIC/Family Systems Instructor for IJR
Chicago, IL

Feminism, Community, and Communication

Journal of Feminist Family Therapy
Volume 11, Number 4

CONTENTS

Introduction: A Patchwork Quilt   1
Mary E. Olson

A Communal Perspective for Relational Therapies   5
Lynn Hoffman

> This paper proposes a framework for postmodern therapies which focuses on the communal creation of meaning. The therapist is both a weaver and a thread, singular, yet one of many. Just as family therapists took advantage of a newly seen unit, the family, to enlarge their range of choices, so can postmodern therapists take advantage of the shift to the non-essentialist position of social construction theory. However, even that theory takes a back seat to a heightened interest in practice. Instead of asking, "What are the philosophical underpinnings of our work," we ask, "What is the knit one, purl two of the kind of social weaving preferred by effective therapists of any school?" The nature of these more communal practices is considered within the historical context of the family therapy field.
>
> KEYWORDS. Postmodern, social construction, communal practices

In Search of Subjugated Knowledge   19
Ann Hartman

Listening to the Voices of Anorexia:
The Researcher as an "Outsider-Witness"   25
Mary E. Olson

> This paper is based on a collaborative research inquiry with women who were formerly anorectic. Drawing on histories of female fasting, feminist cultural criticism, and women's psychology, the study examines the themes of voice and communication and develops relational research practices that allow a person to experience herself as whole. Reflexive and narrative ideas and conversational practices from family therapy are incorporated into an intensive case study method. Since the research proved beneficial to the participants, it may have important implications for more effective forms of therapy.
>
> KEYWORDS. Anorexia, narrative therapy, female fasting, communication, voice, body

Nobody Tells You Who You Are: First Notes on a Community
Project for Girls and Women in Rural Massachusetts 47
Ellen Pulleyblank

> In spite of many changes for girls and women, research indicates that between the ages of nine and twelve many girls begin to limit their expectations. This is often exacerbated in rural areas where girls have few opportunities. This paper provides the first notes about a rural community project for girls and women. It is a description of a community development process that not only addresses the needs of the girls and the adult women mentors who participate, but also of a network of activities and resources developed by and for the larger community.
>
> KEYWORDS. Women's psychology, community building, rural, girls' development, female adolescence, mentoring programs

Can You Love Them Enough?
Organizational Consulting as a Spiritual Quest 65
Patricia Romney

> This paper describes the labor of the heart for those consulting on contested terrain. A loving practice, it is suggested, can sustain the consultant and potentially heal the organization.
>
> KEYWORDS. Black love, organizational consulting, spirituality

The Talking Oppression Blues: Including the Experience
of Power/Powerlessness in the Teaching
of "Cultural Sensitivity" 83
N. Norma Akamatsu

Theorizing Culture: Narrative Ideas and Practice Principles 99
Joan Laird

Ritual as Therapy, Therapy as Ritual 115
Judith Davis

> This article comments on the relationship between ritual and therapy with an exploration of two rituals, one from public life and one from clinical practice. Part one focuses on the bar/bat mitzvah ritual (coming-of-age ceremony for 13 year old Jewish adolescents) as a naturally occurring "therapeutic opportunity," and part two, on the way several leading therapists have used variations on the theme of ritual ceremony to create their unique formats for therapy. In particular, Michael White's use of Barbara Myerhoff's (1986) idea of "definitional ceremony," and Lynn Hoffman's use of Tom Andersen's (1987) "reflecting team" idea are highlighted. An illustrative case story is presented and the article ends with a review of parallels between ritual and therapy.
>
> KEYWORDS. Communal practices, bar/bat mitzvah, ritual, therapy, ceremony, reflecting team

Feminism in the Middle East: Reflections
on Ethnographic Research in Lebanon   131
Catherine K. Kikoski

There is a history of feminism that is rooted in the Middle East. And there is a future. Patriarchy, tradition and religious conservatism in the area have led women to struggle for emancipation and equality on many levels. This ethnographic research study in the Middle East gives voice to a young generation of women who reveal their own unique brand of feminism. The overarching theme of this research seems to be a universal yearning of women to be free to express themselves, and to realize their goals and dreams in their own ways, and in their own cultural contexts. They have a clear vision of themselves in their society, and the role they must play to realize their vision: to lead more autonomous lives, but not at the price of the relationships that sustain and nourish them. In this way, culture punctuates feminism.

KEYWORDS. Lebanon, feminism, ethnography, Middle East

INTERVIEWS

An Interview with Janine Roberts   147
Catherine Weigel Foy

BOOK REVIEWS

Latino Families in Therapy: A Guide to Multicultural Practice,
by Celia Jaes Falicov   159
Reviewed by Veronica Barenstein

Gay and Lesbian Couples: Voices from Lasting Relationships,
by Richard A. Mackey, Bernard A. O'Brien,
and Eileen E. Mackey   164
Reviewed by Gary Sanders

Why History Matters: Life and Thought, by Gerda Lerner   165
Reviewed by Lois Braverman

ABOUT THE GUEST EDITOR

Mary E. Olson, PhD, LICSW, is on the faculty of Smith College School for Social Work and a research associate at its Center for Innovative Practice. She has a private practice in Northampton, MA. From 1990-1995, she was the Director of the Clinical Externship in Systemic Family Therapy at Berkshire Medical Center, Pittsfield, MA. She has consulted with schools, community mental health agencies, and HMOs on a variety of topics including narrative practices, the reflecting process, and writing in therapy. She has published articles on voice and writing, metaphor and therapy, and teaching feminist family therapy. A member of the American Academy of Family Therapists, she holds degrees in literature from Wellesley College and Columbia University, a master's degree from Smith College School for Social Work, and a doctorate in communication from the University of Massachusetts. Her research interest is the interplay of voice, communication, and the body.

Introduction: A Patchwork Quilt

Mary E. Olson

This collection is a patchwork quilt composed by a group of women who call themselves "The Fortune Cookies." We have met regularly for ten years and share similar interests in family therapy, gender, and postmodern ideas. My original concept for the work was that it would represent new areas of creativity that members of our group have developed separately, yet together. This broad canopy appealed to the current editor who is interested in new sources of vitality. It also fit well with an interview planned with Janine Roberts, a former editor of the *Journal of Feminist Family Therapy*, who was one of the first family-therapy trainers in our area.

As the work began to take shape, I saw that there were clear, connecting themes. All of our papers have in common the "social construction of identity" within a "different voice." Each paper highlights the forms of communication in which a positive sense of identity may be constituted and negotiated. Our papers deal with the issues of gender, race, class, culture and religion, which have provided a needed and important corrective to the earlier blind spots of the family field. But, the spirit of these writings seems to me distinct with a renewed emphasis on collaboration, intersubjectivity, and the process of community. These ideas are relevant wherever people interact--in therapy, community work, teaching and research.

I had another unifying association to this set of papers–the cultural concept of communication. John Carey (1988), a communication scholar in the tradi-

---

Mary E. Olson, PhD, LICSW, is Adjunct Professor, Smith College School for Social Work, and a Research Fellow at its Center for Innovative Practice. She has a private practice in Northampton, MA.

Address correspondence to: Mary E. Olson, 151 Main Street, Northampton, MA 01060.

[Haworth co-indexing entry note]: "Introduction: A Patchwork Quilt." Olson, Mary, E. Co-published simultaneously in *Journal of Feminist Family Therapy* (The Haworth Press, Inc.) Vol. 11, No. 4, 2000, pp. 1-4; and: *Feminism, Community, and Communication* (ed: Mary E. Olson) The Haworth Press, Inc., 2000, pp. 1-4. Single or multiple copies of this article are available for a fee from The Haworth Document Delivery Service [1-800-342-9678, 9:00 a.m. - 5:00 p.m. (EST). E-mail address: getinfo@haworthpressinc.com].

© 2000 by The Haworth Press, Inc. All rights reserved.

tion of John Dewey, reminds us of the common roots of the words, "communication," "community," and "communion." Carey argues that the dominant transmission view of communication in the social sciences and in American culture is one that fails to connect people, while the ritual or cultural view makes communication a form of participation. Broadly speaking, I think these papers fall into a cultural perspective where problems of communication, which includes social identity, are tied up with problems of community, and vice versa.

Carey (1988) goes on to say that the transmission view defines communication as "[the geographical extension of] messages in space for the control of distance and people" (p. 15). Giving his opinion that the roots of European colonization lie in the idea of the New World as a religious project, Carey says that the mission of the early Christian settlers was to "transmit" the Word to the Americas, especially to the native peoples. Colonization occurred in the name of establishing and enlarging the Kingdom of God. As American culture subsequently became secular, and as technology became linked to the idea of progress, communication continued to be seen as the transmission and retrieval of information, with a residual overtone as a positive good.

By contrast, Carey states that a totally different theory of communication originates from the world of speech. This alternate view focuses on a different order of experience where the communicative universe is understood not as the transmission of messages but as membership in a social network. The metaphors of ritual, ceremony, dance, and performance provide more appropriate analogs for human experience, because they connect communication to the shared process of making and remaking social worlds.

Carey (1988) goes on to make the point that the cultural view of communication in America derives historically from the town hall meetings and religious ceremonies that bring people together in common purpose. These aspects of sacred and civic life influenced the nineteenth-century philosophical worldview that came to be known as American pragmatism. The major scholars within this tradition of social thought include John Dewey, who drew his metaphors for communication from speech, and the thinkers whom he influenced, who range from George Herbert Mead to Erving Goffman. Contemporary sponsors of this view are the social constructionists–Thomas Kuhn, Peter Berger, Thomas Luckmann, Clifford Geertz, Kenneth Gergen, John Shotter, Barnett Pearce and Vernon Cronen. Although coming from a different transatlantic tradition, postmodern European voices such as Mikhail Bakhtin and Michel Foucault articulate a conception of communication akin to that of the American pragmatists. They all agree that language and communication constitute symbolic activities whereby social reality is produced, maintained, stabilized, and transformed.

Under the overlapping influences of postmodernism and social construction theory, all the contributors to this work show how, within different contexts, communication works as a world-making and identity-making activity. Lynn Hoffman's paper on a "communal perspective" describes how therapists undertake to "rebuild local worlds" mainly by acts of listening and understanding rather than stating and knowing. She writes about the work of other women in the field–Virginia Satir, Harlene Anderson, and Peggy Penn–although this perspective is not limited to women. Tom Andersen's reflecting team, Michael White's community of concern, Chris Kinman's collaborative action plan, and Marcelo Pakman's critical social practice are ideas that are also woven into this view that Lynn says "defies borders."

Ann Hartman's prescient essay on social work–as timely today as when it was first published in 1992–also calls attention to the ethic of listening. Ann sees this stance as the cornerstone of "the collaborative search for meaning" between the practitioner or researcher and the person to be understood. The aim here is understanding, not imposing professional formulations and thus colonizing the experience of those whom we try to know.

My paper, too, is based on a collaborative research inquiry I did with women who were formerly anorectic. From the position of an "outsider witness," I examine the themes of voice and communication and develop relational research practices that allow a person to experience herself as a living, vocal self. In another project, one that incorporates recent research on women and girls, Ellen Pulleyblank writes about "Sisters Inc.," an effort to build a "hardiness zone" for girls in the Hilltowns of Western Massachusetts. She describes how she uses mentoring relationships and visual arts to create resilience and connection. This paper illustrates how community building can be placed in the service of an effective relational psychology.

Pat Romney's, "Can You Love them Enough?" emphasizes the power of love and spirituality in her work as an organizational consultant to an agency beset by fierce racial divides. Her thinking provides a sharp contrast to the adversarial contests that so often surround such trainings in agencies stratified by race and class. Norma Akamatsu, facing another divided social field, uses "thick conversation" to open the space for what she calls "multiple social identities in deadlocked either/or conversations." Her paper explores a way to counteract divisive controversies within the professional world.

Joan Laird's paper challenges the conventional notion of culture as transmitted and argues instead for culture as "performed," "improvised," "fluid," and "emergent." "Each performance [of ourselves]" she says, "is a combination of tradition and imagination." Judy Davis does the same by comparing the transforming ceremony of therapy to the public theater of the Bar/Bat Mitzvah. For her, both therapy and ritual are performance arts. Imbued with a similar respect for culture, Catherine Kikoski writes about an ethnographic research project where she interviewed young Lebanese women about their lives and, while listening to their stories, saw evidence of critical cultural change.

These papers represent a way of thinking and doing therapy, research, community work, and organizational consulting that highlights the ethical dimension. Each one assumes that human beings are makers of meaning within a common world, rather than objects to be scrutinized by an expert. Relationship, voice, agency, and community are themes inherent in this work. While such ideas themselves are not new, my sister scholar-therapists have taken them in a new direction.

The process of writing these papers and collecting them in a single work has given our group a new sense of purpose. We have worked hard to bring this patchwork quilt to completion, often filling in stitches for each other. As a first-time editor, I wish to thank all the Cookies for their spirit, interest, and energy. Let me end with a remark by Lynn Hoffman: "A fortune cookie is the only cookie with a text inside."

REFERENCES

Carey, J. W. (1988). *Communication as culture: Essays on media and society.* Boston: Unwin Hyman

A Communal Perspective for Relational Therapies

Lynn Hoffman

SUMMARY. This paper proposes a framework for postmodern therapies which focuses on the communal creation of meaning. The therapist is both a weaver and a thread, singular, yet one of many. Just as family therapists took advantage of a newly seen unit, the family, to enlarge their range of choices, so can postmodern therapists take advantage of the shift to the non-essentialist position of social construction theory. However, even that theory takes a back seat to a heightened interest in practice. Instead of asking, "What are the philosophical underpinnings of our work," we ask, "What is the knit one, purl two of the kind of social weaving preferred by effective therapists of any school?" The nature of these more communal practices is considered within the historical context of the family therapy field. *[Article copies available for a fee from The Haworth Document Delivery Service: 1-800-342-9678. E-mail address: <getinfo@haworthpressinc.com> Website: <http://www.haworthpressinc.com>]*

KEYWORDS. Postmodern, social construction, communal practices

INTRODUCTION

Systemic therapy, as a genre, and constructivism, as its philosophy, has been the bridge that connects the modern, essentialist framework of tradition-

---

Lynn Hoffman, MSW, is on the faculty of the Marriage and Family Therapy Program at Saint Joseph College.

Address correspondence to: Lynn Hoffman, 151 Main St., Northampton, MA 01060.

[Haworth co-indexing entry note]: "A Communal Perspective for Relational Therapies." Hoffman, Lynn. Co-published simultaneously in *Journal of Feminist Family Therapy* (The Haworth Press, Inc.) Vol. 11, No. 4, 2000, pp. 5-17; and: *Feminism, Community, and Communication* (ed: Mary E. Olson) The Haworth Press, Inc., 2000, pp. 5-17. Single or multiple copies of this article are available for a fee from The Haworth Document Delivery Service [1-800-342-9678, 9:00 a.m. - 5:00 p.m. (EST). E-mail address: getinfo@haworthpressinc.com].

al family therapy to the postmodern constructionist one. The difference between these positions is neatly summed up in the story of the Three Umpires:

> First Umpire: I calls 'em as they are. (essentialism)
> Second Umpire: I calls 'em as I sees 'em. (constructivism)
> Third Umpire: They ain't nothing till I calls 'em. (constructionism)

Translated for the purposes of therapy, the essentialist looks for the cause of the problem and tries to fix it. The problem exists in the real world "out there." Constructivist therapists disagree. They say we can't know what is out there, even though it may exist, because what we perceive is always filtered through cognitive and sensory screens. That is why Maturana always started a lecture by drawing an observing eye in the upper right hand corner of the blackboard.

The constructionist therapist moves to the social web. Feeling herself to be part of a tapestry woven from elements like language, customs and culture, she is at the same time one of the weavers and one of the threads. Kenneth Gergen (1994), the chief proponent of social construction theory, speaks in the same way of the communal creation of meaning. Having taken up a constructionist position myself, I have been exploring the dimensions of this communal perspective and the practices that fall naturally out of it.

But let me start with where family therapy in the U.S. is now. Managed care, with its demands for accountability, has pushed the field of family therapy up against the wall. Many of us are asking what, if anything, backs up our claims. Research results are not outstanding, in part because many of our approaches don't emphasize outcomes, but also because studies of family therapy results are not compelling (Shadish et al., 1995).

Worse yet, we don't even agree on what kind of issues family therapy should deal with. Starting modestly with schizophrenia, we moved on to parent-child problems, marital woes, developmental traumas, life stage stuckness, gender discrimination, sexual abuse, violence, addiction, poverty, and all the injustices of class, ethnicity and race. At the same time, the competition between the "helping professions" for the right to treat these woes has intensified.

This seemed like a good time to assess the field. Even though I am not in the same place where I started, I didn't want to abandon all the good ideas I learned on the way. So I tried to think of family therapy as a braided Easter bread, or (in the Jewish tradition) a Challah, with strands from early on disappearing and then reappearing in a changed position or on another side. Each new strand suggested an answer to a question that had been brought to the fore by a previous one. However, it was the continuing conversation between the strands that made the entire braid so special.

THE EARLY STRANDS

In a recent article (Hoffman, 1998), I described the influence of psychodynamic ideas on early family therapy, citing psychologist Margaret Singer's (1996) view that the ascendance of psychoanalytic and developmental theories after World War II rested on an etiological framework. Singer and others have called this view the "blame and change game." If you can find someone to blame, you can change. Instead of the finger being pointed at the inner dynamics of the individual, it was pointed at some outside influence or person instead.

Early family therapy developed a blame and change game of its own. Family researchers ascribed the cause of emotional distress to underlying factors like unacknowledged anger or unexpressed grief. These conditions, like festering sores, needed to be exposed to light and air. From early on, the key example was the idea that the symptoms of the child hid the parents' pain. Once the therapist focused on the marital conflict, it was thought that the child's symptoms would disappear. This paralleled the psychoanalytic belief that symptoms were surface manifestations of a deeper wound.

This position was usually benign in individual therapy, because the people who were implicitly most at fault remained outside, but it had a chilling effect on family therapy with the whole family because these guilty ones were present. At first, mothers were to blame. Then therapists zeroed in on the parents, who were seen as "triangling" the child into their own conflicts. The collateral kin group was next focused on, then the other helpers who might be entangled in a case. As time went by, the lens steadily widened, but the blame remained.

The notable exception to this perspective was the Mental Research Institute's Interactional View (Watzlawick, Weakland and Fisch, 1974). Drawing on Milton Erickson's hypnotherapy (Haley, 1973), the MRI group ignored causes and took a rhetorical approach instead. Being constructivists, they held that reality is constructed, and that it was the therapist's job to shape it differently. Strikingly, the MRI never targeted any treatment unit except the complaint, and never insisted the whole family be called in.

The downside of this approach was its condescending view of the customer. Family therapy was likened to a game of chess. The therapist, who knew the rules of the game, was the master player, while the family members were the pieces on the board. An approach like this would naturally tend to hide the thinking behind its moves. If the customer knew the reason for maneuvers like paradoxical interventions, this could undermine their success. One had an extraordinary sense of a band of therapists conducting guerilla warfare against customers determined to resist them.

A new strand then appeared that blended etiological and rhetorical elements together. For the Milan Systemic team (Selvini-Palazzoli et al., 1978), the cause of psychosis in children was a double-binding family constellation that Selvini called an "imbrolio." However, their chief intervention was rhetorical: a "counterparadox" that prescribed the relationship system that supposedly maintained the symptom. True to the group's research orientation, all interviews were watched by a team behind a screen and videotaped, to be studied later. This team idea fascinated therapists and was widely imitated, but it put a gulf between them and their clients and turned the one-way mirror into a one-way street.

Luigi Boscolo and Gianfranco Cecchin (1987) then broke away to start their own training center. The invention of "circular questioning" (Selvini et al., 1980) gave Milan-style therapists a tool for placing family members in a position to reflect on the machinery they were caught in. Cecchin (1996) moved off in this direction, as did practitioners like Karl Tomm (1987). As a result, the pejorative "systemic hypothesis" began to be replaced by reflexive conversations that did not necessarily imply innocence or guilt.

The Interactional approach of the MRI mutated too. Steve de Shazer and Insoo Berg (1991, 1994), along with colleagues like Ben Furman (1992), Eve Lipchik (1993), and William O'Hanlon (1989), moved from an emphasis on problems to an emphasis on solutions. Berg and de Shazer called this a Solution-Focused approach. Solution-talk, despite being just as rhetorical as the problem-talk of the MRI, looked at possibility rather than pathology and had a vastly more sympathetic feel.

These developments were shifts in a more collaborative direction. However, an even more seismic movement called Postmodernism was threatening the pillars that held them up. Instead of asking, "What is the 'thing in the bushes?'" (Hoffman, 1981), we asked, "How do our ways of knowing create the thing in the bushes? How do intellectual frameworks like normative science constrain what we can know?" For me, this was a watershed. I had never stepped outside the assumptions of my education on so large a scale before.

THE INFLUENCE OF POSTMODERNISM

I think it is correct to call Postmodernism a true paradigm shift. Paradigms are explanatory systems that shape the sensibility of large communities of knowers, in our case the Anglo-European knowers of the Western World. Every once in a while these frameworks wear out, and then all the little sub-fields that dangle from them need to change too. Instead of believing in stationary unities such as the "self," the "family," "nature," we began to question them. As philosopher Richard Rorty (1980) says:

> The picture which holds traditional philosophy captive is that of the mind as a great mirror containing various representations–some accu-

rate, some not, and capable of being studied by pure nonempirical methods. Without the notion of mind as mirror, the notion of knowledge as accuracy of presentation would not have suggested itself. (p. 12)

In the course of this revolution, academic, scientific and professional certitudes were placed, as the French philosopher Jacques Derrida (1976) would say, "under erasure." Also under erasure were the "Western Canon" that was founded on the "Great Books," and the "Dead White Men" who wrote them. Critical feminists like Rachel Hare-Mustin (1994) began to prod family therapists about their blindness to gender and race and asked a pointed question: must all our therapy discourses be kept within the "mirrored rooms?"

Particular scorn was heaped on the white males of family therapy. In *The Family Interpreted* (1988), Deborah Luepnitz took issue with the psychiatrists who were family therapy's pioneers, and questioned the teaching of philosopher kings like Gregory Bateson. Systemic therapists were particularly attacked for blaming women; for leaving out questions of power; and for ignoring issues of social justice (Erickson, 1988). It became clear that the "ecosystems" metaphor made the rights of individuals subservient to the balance of the whole.

But I was struggling with other concerns. In "Beyond Power and Control" (1985), I tried to offer an alternative to the masculinist discourse of family therapy. I wanted to make available what psychologist Carol Gilligan (1984) had called a "different voice." I did not think that this different voice belonged to women, only that the authoritative stance of the expert should not be the only one. But the prevailing wisdom framed what was then called "difference feminism" in a very negative light. It was the right article at the wrong time.

Thanks to postmodern philosopher Lois Shawver (1998), I recently discovered an ally in French philosopher Jean-Francois Lyotard. In *Just Gaming* (1985), he compares the competitive "game of speculation" of the Western philosophical tradition to the "game without an author," in which the purpose is to listen and understand. He says this amazing thing:

> For us, a language is first and foremost someone talking. But there are language games in which the important thing is to listen, in which the rule deals with audition. Such a game is the game of the just. And in this game, one speaks as a listener, and not as an author. It is a game without an author, in the same way as the speculative game of the West is a game without a listener, because the only listener tolerated by the speculative philosopher is the disciple. (p. 71)

These passages, which I did not know about when I wrote my article, give it a retrospective credibility. If therapy fits into Lyotard's category of the "game without an author," this realization becomes an additional context for Anderson and Goolishian's later (1988) concept of "not knowing." However, for the next few years, the playing field became increasingly concerned with the contests that took place around identity politics, and my idea of a different voice seemed not to fit.

What did fit was an approach to therapy that called itself "Narrative" and broke sharply with the traditional family systems view. The originators of this approach, Michael White and David Epston (1995), were deeply impressed by Jerome Bruner's (1990) invention of Cultural Psychology. Illustrating the ubiquity of cultural blind spots, Bruner tells a story about the anthropologist Edward Evans-Pritchard. While he was interviewing his African informants about their religious beliefs, one of them pointed to "the divinity he wore on his wrist," which Pritchard seemed to consult "whenever he made a decision." Bruner's mandate for cultural awareness was supported by the growing sensitivity to multicultural issues of the '90s.

White and Epston were also influenced by the ideas of social philosopher Michel Foucault (1984). Foucault (1972) had brilliantly outed the oppressive cultural discourses of everyday life and White and Epston applied his thinking to many problems, from anorexia to family violence. By using a rhetorical technique they called "externalizing," they found a way to align themselves with the person against the personified problem, whatever it might be. This strategy allowed them to put moral agency back into family therapy, a great relief to many after the neutral stance of the systemic years.

In an interesting move away from the modern/postmodern dichotomy, White has set up another one which covers much the same territory: structuralism vs. poststructuralism. Structuralism seems to be similar to "essentialism" in that both concepts assume that there is a hidden essence or structure within the unit or event being described. On the surface it feels less pejorative to be dismissed as a structuralist than as a modernist. But there is still an Us vs. Them implication in both postmodernism and poststructuralism which we would do well not to ignore.

There is a similar drawback to the Foucauldian vision: a world is evoked like the one in Margaret Atwood's (1992) *The Handmaid's Tale*. Its defining parameters are imprisonment, surveillance, and resistance. In the wrong hands, this polarizing language could easily become another blame and change game. However, White has moved in the opposite direction. His interviewing style has become much less hard-edged. Early on, the externalizing questions gave the impression of sheep dogs herding their charges into the little corral. Now he takes seriously his own advice to "stay one step behind." As a result, an unprecedented tenderness pervades his work.

A second postmodern strand, called a Collaborative Language Systems approach, came out of the teamwork of the late Harry Goolishian and Harlene

Anderson (1997). This view looks for support to linguistic philosophers like Ludwig Wittgenstein (1963) and Mikhail Bakhtin (1984), and to social constructionists like Kenneth Gergen (1994) and John Shotter (1990). In applying postmodern theory to therapy, Anderson believes that the critical piece is that the therapist come from a place of "not knowing." As a result, she goes directly to the persons who consult her, asking what their own opinions are and what they feel would be useful. For her, solutions can only be arrived at from within the therapeutic conversation, through a process of what she calls "mutual puzzling."

Extending this position, John Lannaman's recent article in *Family Process* (1999) moves away from a linguistic metaphor to one derived from physical embodiment and touch. I am extremely sympathetic to this view. The notion of sublingual communication, which I see as the underground rivers of sensed feelings that flow between people when they connect, describes the process of our work much better than the more remote analogies of narrative and text. In my 1998 article, I compare therapy to the process of kneading yeast bread. The reason I like this metaphor is that it fits with Wittgenstein's (1953) idea that the speaking of language is part of an activity or "form of life."

Don Schoen supports this view in his wonderful book *The Reflective Practitioner* (1984). He says that the actual practice of therapy should be the source of one's knowledge about it, and this is why it is so important to watch at first hand what self-styled postmodern therapists actually do. Their interviews contrast sharply with those of essentialist and constructivist family therapists. There are no lists of questions, no interviewing guidelines, no interventions, no goals. Constructionist therapists refrain from going into therapy with a blueprint of any kind. But they do attempt to influence the atmosphere in which therapy takes place by presiding over the equivalent of a virtual quilting bee. Looking for a descriptive phrase, I turned to the idea of "communal practices."

COMMUNAL PRACTICES

In *Realities and Relationships* (1994), Gergen links the word "communality" with social interaction. Observing that the traditional view that meaning originates within the individual mind is deeply problematic, he goes on to say:

> Words (or texts) within themselves bear no meaning; they fail to communicate. They only appear to generate meaning by virtue of their place within the realm of human interaction. It is human interchange that gives language its capacity to mean, and it must stand as the critical

locus of concern. I wish then to replace *textuality* with *communality*. This shift allows us to restructure much that has been said about meaning within texts as a commentary on *forms of relatedness*. (p. 263-4)

It was Tom Andersen, however, who first used the phrase "communal perspective" to describe a stance toward therapy. He had asked me to do a workshop on that subject in Norway in 1999. I had long been brooding on the subtle communicational weaving that I saw in Andersen's reflecting teams. It was not the reflections themselves that so impressed me but the fact that one group would comment on what another group said, and yet another group would comment in turn, creating a juxtaposition out of which surprising meanings could arise. My phrase for this process was "knit one, purl two." Michael White calls it "telling and re-telling." Now I think of it more generally as a "communal practice."

This type of practice always has to do with the relational context of a problem. Modern family therapists tried to change the structure of the "dysfunctional family" directly, believing that it was causing the distress. Constructivist therapists tried to disrupt the vicious cycles that the problem produced, by changing an element in the sequence, or by prescribing it, which often created a recoil. Constructionist therapists stopped thinking of change at all, but moved toward influencing the social atmosphere. This meant doing whatever would counteract the isolation and despair that a problem in a family or network brought with it.

As a result, the work of postmodern therapists goes in the direction of what I think of as "world-building." In *The Timeless Way of Building* (1979), architect Christopher Alexander invokes a time before there were blueprints. He asks himself: "If we have no formal guidelines, what is the central quality we look for when we build?" After much discussion with himself, he finally comes up with "Aliveness." We instinctively know when a house, a garden, a town, is "dead" because we do not want to go there. If it feels alive, we do. He talks about the patterns used before there were architects, patterns that have a folk feel and are intuitive rather than mechanical. Among these he lists "farmhouse kitchen," "child caves," and (for the garden) "sunny corner."

Some of the early family therapists were folk builders in that sense. The person that comes most to mind is Virginia Satir. She was in one sense a constructivist, in that she specialized in pointing out conflicting perceptions of reality. She had a hundred ways to call attention to the "discrepancies," as she called them, that created so many family divides. But Satir was also an early constructionist. Her "reframing" techniques were not so much a way to disarm resistance as a method for softening the way people heard each other. My favorite example (1968) is an interview with the family of a minister and his wife. Their teenage son had impregnated two of his classmates, and was sitting in a corner with his head down. The first thing Satir did on coming into the room was to say to him, "Well, we know one thing. God gave you good seed."

Instead of calling this move "reframing," Lois Shawver (1983) prefers "transvaluation." This term describes a way of changing the significance of a situation, usually from pessimistic to hopeful, but always from an expected to an unexpected point of view. I like Shawver's term because it embraces a shift that, even if suggested by the therapist, does not exempt her from the experience of change. And the source of the transvaluation may be any person present. Unlike "reframing," which is a strategy that can be learned by rote and is imposed by the therapist, it arises spontaneously from the conversation.

Looking back at Satir's work gave me a new perception of Tom Andersen's (1990) invention of the reflecting team. The "reflecting process," as Andersen later called it, gave concrete form to the overhearing position, as opposed to the observing position of every other approach to therapy I had known. It turned out that a reflecting conversation could be applied to many settings: teaching, supervision, mediation, workshops, even conferences. Like the legendary little black dress, you could dress it up or dress it down, it could go anywhere.

In fact, the reflecting team changed therapy as I knew it. Wherever it went, it brought connection. As soon as I began to use it, a more horizontal relationship sprang up between me and the people who came to see me. It turned opposing voices into parallel voices. It allowed the therapist to decenter herself. The "therapeutic boundary" began to melt and interventions became a thing of the past. Most amazing of all, the atmosphere of the session became intent and focused, as if we were all experiencing the pull of a good mystery story. In truth, we were often rewarded by a denouement of unexpected beauty and force.

The effect of these conversations was to make people feel understood and to create hope. Most therapeutic procedures involve putting people in the wrong: diagnosing their faults, blaming their relatives, casting doubt on their upbringing. The virtue of the reflecting process is the way it can build "a good city" in a very special sense: by creating an ad hoc community where people can feel (my words) more safe, more free, and more alive.

White, too, has gone in a communal direction (Hoffman, 1998). Citing Meyerhoff's (1982) idea of definitional ceremonies, he started using the format of the reflecting team as a source of "outsider witnesses," people whose words could enrich the stories of the persons who consulted him. As part of this enterprise, he conscripts workshop participants or brings in individuals from a person's natural environment, in spirit or in life. Through these ceremonies of "telling and re-telling," White tries to create "thicker descriptions" for the people who are present to overhear.

I call this the Lake Titicaca Effect. High up in the Andes Mountains of Peru is a lake surrounded by reeds. My mother was the first person I ever knew who had seen this lake, because she had gone to South America in 1942 to study the woven fabrics of the Mayan people. When the people there build a house, they lay reeds on top of reeds until there is a floating platform six feet thick. They use the same reeds for their houses, and I think their boats as well. The Reflecting Team, or as Andersen now calls it the "reflecting process," works the same way, by creating a deeply connected platform on which a house or village can be built.

Peggy Penn is a communal therapist in this same sense. She encourages the people who consult her to write: journals, letters, autobiography, poems—with the hope of enlarging their worlds or mending their safety nets. In a recent article (1998), a young rape victim is plagued by flashbacks of her shocking experience. Penn asks which persons might have made a difference had they been available to protect her. The woman answers that her husband might have been such a presence. Penn suggests that the woman imagine him coming into her flashbacks as a protector. Previously, the woman had seen her husband only as a bystander, but by including him in this new way, she created a zone of safety for herself.

The work of these postmodern therapists often includes tears. Traditional family therapists encouraged "affect" in order to help family members to experience repressed emotions, even though they themselves never showed emotion or disclosed anything personal. But postmodern practitioners will tell stories from their own lives. They will practice what I used to call, and hide from my supervisor, "corny therapy." In the old days, a therapist would hold out the kleenex box to a client. In these newer days, the therapist will weep right along with her.

I would like to mention two more practitioners who, though not using this term, work in communal ways. Marcelo Pakman (1998) is a psychiatrist of the disenfranchised. Calling what he does "critical social practice," he often links the people who come to see him with others. A man comes to him, upset becauses he sees his mother's face as "deformed." He believes this is the work of the FBI. Pakman asks him to select someone in the waiting room who looks sympathetic, and tell him about his worries, but not to mention the FBI. The man says to him, "You're odd," but complies. When the man comes back, Pakman asks what happened. The man says, "The person I spoke to told me that my mother is old and ill." After that, whenever he sees Pakman in the day hospital, he repeats, "You're odd."

The other communal worker, Chris Kinman (1996), uses concepts like generosity and abundance in consulting to families from First Nations communities in Vancouver, B.C. Kinman seeks to replace "problem" language with "gift" languages. In assessing an individual's situation, Kinman has devised what he calls a "Collaborative Action Plan," which poses questions about "gifts," "potentials," "roadblocks" and "community contributions." And twice he has asked me out to Vancouver to take part in the sort of event he calls "Honoring Community," a reflecting conversation with local groups that work with children.

Communal practices like these make up a category that defies borders. As I said, many so-called modern therapists use them; postmodern therapists do too, but with more self-consciousness. But there is one irreversible advance that comes with postmodernism: an awareness of the limitations of knowing. In a recent paper (1999), Fred Newman describes postmodern therapy as a study of the unknowable, meaning the domain of things that cannot be discovered in the same way that things in the physical universe can. For this reason, he states that storytelling should not be turned into a kind of explanation but should be seen instead as "a non-explanatory mode of understanding the activity of human life."

I like that idea. I want to continue to be "not knowing" at the level of the road map while still exploring the road. If you are like me, you will remember the sand tunnels we used to dig as children at the beach, and that delicious final moment when our fingers touched.

REFERENCES

Alexander, C. (1979) *The Timeless Way of Building.* New York: Oxford University Press.
Andersen, T. (ed) (1990) *The Reflecting Team: Dialogues and Dialogues about the Dialogues.* Broadstairs, Kent: Borgmann.
Anderson, H., and Goolishian, H. (1988) "Human Systems As Linguistic Systems." *Family Process* 27, 371-93.
Anderson, H. (1997) *Language, Conversation and Possibilities.* New York: Basic Books.
Atwood, M. (1992) *The Handmaid's Tale.* New York: Doubleday.
Bakhtin, M. (1981) *The Dialogical Imagination.* M. Holquist (ed.) and C. Emerson (tr.), Minneapolis: University of Minneapolis Press.
Berg, I.K. (1994) *Family Based Services: A Solution-Focused Approach.* New York: W.W. Norton.
Boscolo, L., Cecchin, G., Hoffman, L. and Penn, P. (1987) *Milan Systemic Family Therapy.* New York: Basic Books.
Bruner, J. (1990) *Acts of Meaning.* Cambridge, MA: Harvard University Press, p. 37.
Cecchin, G. and Lane, G. (1991) *Irreverence: A Strategy for Therapist Survival.* London: Karnac Books.
de Shazer, S. (1985) *Keys to Solution in Brief Therapy.* New York: W.W. Norton.
Furman, B., and T. Ahola (1992) *Solution Talk.* New York: W.W. Norton.
Foucault, M. (1972) *The Archeology of Knowlege,* New York: Pantheon.
Gergen, K. (1994) *Realities and Relationships.* Cambridge, MA: University of Harvard Press.

Gilligan, C. (1982) *In a Different Voice.* Cambridge, MA: Harvard University Press.
Goodman, N. (1978) *Ways of Worldmaking.* New York: Hackett.
Haley, J. (1973) *The Uncommon Therapy of Milton Erickson.* New York: W.W. Norton.
Hare-Mustin, R. (1994) "Discourses in the Mirrored Room." *Family Process* 33, 19-35.
Hoffman, L. (1981) *Foundations of Family Therapy.* New York: Basic Books.
Hoffman, L. (1985) "Beyond Power and Control." *Family Systems Medicine,* 3, 381-396.
Hoffman, L. (1998) "Setting Aside the Model in Family Therapy." *Journal of Marital and Family Therapy,* 24, 145-156.
Kinman, C. (1996) *Honouring Community.* Abbotsford, B.C: Fraser Valley Education & Therapy Services.
Lannaman, J. (1999) "Social Construction and Materiality," *Family Process,* 37, 393-413.
Lipchik, E. (1993) "Both/And Solutions." In S. Friedman (ed), *The New Language Of Change.* New York: Guilford Press
Luepnitz, D. (1988) *The Family Interpreted.* New York: Basic Books.
Lyotard, J-F. (1989) One Thing at Stake in Women's Struggles." In *The Lyotard Reader.* New York: Basil Blackwell, Inc.
Lyotard, J-F. and J-L. Thebaud, (1996) *Just Gaming* (tr. Wlad Godzich). Minneapolis: Minnesota University Press.
Maturana, H. and Varela, F. (1980) *Autopoiesis and Cognition.* Dordrecht, Holland: D. Reidel.
Myerhoff, B. (1986) "Life Not Death In Venice." In Turner, V. and Bruner, E. (eds), *The Anthropology of Experience.* Chicago: University of Illinois Press.
Newman, F. (1999) "Does a Story Need a Theory?" In Fee, D. (Ed.) *Pathology and the Postmodern: Mental Illness as Discourse and Experience.* London: Sage Publications.
Pakman. M. (1999) "Designing Constructive Therapies in Mental Health." *Journal of Marital and Family Therapy,* 25, 83-98.
Penn, P. (1998) "Rape Flashbacks: Constructing a New Narrative." *Family Process,* 37, 299-310
Satir, V. (1967) "A Family of Angels." In J. Haley and L. Hoffman (eds.) *Techniques of Family Therapy,* New York: Basic Books.
Schoen, D. (1984) *The Reflective Practitioner.* New York: Basic Books.
Selvini-Palazzoli, M., Boscolo, L., Prata, G., and Cecchin, G. (1978) *Paradox and Counterparadox.* New York: Jason Aronson
Selvini-Palazzoli, M. et. al. (1980) "Hypothesizing-Circularity-Neutrality." *Family Process* 19, 3-12.
Shadish, W. et. al. (1995) "The Efficacy and Effectiveness of Marital and Family Therapy." *Family Process,* 21, 345-360.
Shawver, L. (1983) "Harnessing the Power of Interpretive Language." *Psychotherapy: Theory, Research and Practice,* 20, 3-11.
Shawver, L. (1998), On the Clinical Relevance of Selected Postmodern Ideas: with a Focus on Lyotard's Concept of "Differend." *Journal of the American Academy of Psychoanalysis,* 26 (4), 617-635.

Shotter, J. (1993) *The Cultural Politics of Everyday Life.* Toronto: University of Toronto Press.

Singer, M. (1996) "From Rehabilitation to Etiology: Progress and Pitfalls." In J. Zeig (ed), *The Evolution of Psychotherapy: The Third Conference.* New York: Brunner/Mazel.

Tomm, K. (1987) "Interventive Interviewing: Part II: Reflexive Questioning as a Means to Enable Self-Healing." *Family Process* 26, 167-183.

Watzlawick, P., Weakland, J. and Fisch, R., (1974) *Change: Principles of Problem Formation and Problem Resolution.* New York: W.W. Norton.

White, M. and Epston, D. (1990) *Narrative Means to Therapeutic Ends.* New York: W.W. Norton.

White, M. (1995) *Re-Authoring Lives,* Adelaide, South Australia: Dulwich Centre Publications.

Wittgenstein, L. (1953) *Philosophical Investigations.* Oxford, Blackwell.

In Search of Subjugated Knowledge

Ann Hartman

I can't say who I am unless you agree I'm real.
—Imamu Amiri Baraka

The above lines simply and eloquently express a vision of knowledge, oppression, power, and truth that have enormous implications for social work practitioners, educators, and researchers. Sharing this poet's vision, postmodern French philosopher Michel Foucault (1980) has taught us that knowledge and power are one, that "we are subjugated to the production of truth through power and we cannot exercise power except through the production of truth" (p. 93).

Social workers, who are deeply concerned about oppressed people, poor people, people of color, women, and people suffering from disabling emotional problems and who are committed to the empowerment of their clients, must examine this intimate power-knowledge relationship. Social workers must reflect on the extent to which we may unwittingly and well meaningly disempower our clients through our role as "expert," through the authority of our knowledge.

Foucault (1980) studied the development and institutionalization of what he termed "global unitary knowledges" that, through a struggle over time, have come to subjugate a whole set of knowledges and disqualify them as "beneath the required level of cognition or scientificity" (p. 82). In his analysis, the

---

Ann Hartman, DSW, is Distinguished Professor, Fordham University Graduate School of Social Service and Professor and Dean Emerita, Smith College School for Social Work.

Address correspondence to: Ann Hartman, Smith College School for Social Work, Lilly Hall, Northampton, MA 01060.

Reprinted with permission from the NASW Press.

[Haworth co-indexing entry note]: "In Search of Subjugated Knowledge." Hartman, Ann. Co-published simultaneously in *Journal of Feminist Family Therapy* (The Haworth Press, Inc.) Vol. 11, No. 4, 2000, pp. 19-23; and: *Feminism, Community, and Communication* (ed: Mary E. Olson) The Haworth Press, Inc., 2000, pp. 19-23.

privileging of the methods of science and unitary knowledges have led to the subjugation of previously established erudite knowledge and of local, popular, indigenous knowledge located at the margins of society. These subjugated knowledges have been exiled from the "legitimate domains of formal knowledge" (White & Epston, 1990, p. 26).

Foucault's concern was not only with the centralized political, economic, and institutional regimes that produce privileged knowledges, but also with their exercise of power in the capillaries as they flow out and are practiced at the local level. Or, as Parker (1989) wrote, "The knowledge that circulates in discourse is employed in everyday interaction in relations of submission and domination" (p. 63).

For example, that powerful global and unitary body of knowledge, the *Diagnostic and Statistical Manual of Mental Disorders,* Third Edition (American Psychiatric Association, 1980), which is centrally established and encoded in economic, medical, and educational systems, is practiced at the most local level–in the relationship between a social worker and a client. When a social worker is required by an agency's funding needs or by the rules of third-party payers to attach a diagnostic label to a client, a powerful and privileged classification system has entered this relationship and in all likelihood has affected the worker's thinking, the relationship, and the client's self-definition.

Foucault's (1980) analysis can, perhaps, best be understood through illustrations. The well-known story of how incest has been understood is a dramatic example. After initially thinking that the cause of emotional disturbance in adult women was their being sexually abused as children, Freud came to believe that such memories reported by women were not of real events but were childhood fantasies, evidence of infantile sexual wishes. This scientific knowledge was so reassuring and served such powerful interests that it was maintained for almost 100 years. It was maintained so successfully that the knowledge of incest victims was subjugated to the extent that victims themselves denied their own experience.

Another example of the hegemony of global, unitary knowledge has been the invisibility of women and of people of color in the social sciences, constructed by white males with a few generally marginalized and quieted alternate voices. Other examples include the definition of homosexuality as a disease with resulting elaborate and even destructive protocols for cure and the widely adopted notion of the schizophrenogenic mother and schizophrenic family.

The political nature of knowledge is well illustrated by the fact that each of these privileged truths has been challenged, not primarily by alternative theories from the sciences but by sociopolitical movements that lead to what Foucault (1980) called the insurrection of subjugated knowledge. The women's movement encouraged women to break silence and tell their stories and stimulated the critique of the theory that incest memories were fantasy. The civil rights movement and the rich flowering of African American literature have begun to make visible the African American experience (Collins, 1990). Modern African American women writers are not only bringing forth current subjugated knowledge but are going back to reclaim the ancient knowledges of long-lost early writers such as Zora Neale Hurston and Maria Stewart. In going back these writers are able to connect the historic and current struggles. Gay and lesbian pride, which was sparked by the Stonewall resistance, potentiated the insurrection of yet another subjugated knowledge and the official depathologizing of homosexuality, if not the eradication of homophobia. The mental patients' rights movements and activism on the part of the families of mentally ill people have led to a revision of the discourse about and treatment of mentally ill people and their families.

In each of these examples, oppressed and marginalized populations whose experiences had been described, defined, and categorized by powerful experts rose up to tell their own stories, to bear witness to their own experience, and to define themselves. Through this process, through this insurrection, they have become empowered; and as they have become empowered, their own truths and their own knowledges have begun to be validated and legitimized.

What does this mean for social work practice and research? How can we avoid participating in oppression? How can we lend our efforts to the insurrection of subjugated knowledge and the empowerment of our marginalized client populations?

First, in research and practice we must abandon the role of expert, we must abandon the notion that we are objective observers and our clients are passive subjects to be described and defined. In Foucault's (1980) words,

> We must entertain the claims to attention of local, discontinuous, disqualified, illegitimate knowledges against the claims of a unitary body of theory which would filter, hierarchize, and order them in the name of some true knowledge and some arbitrary idea of what constitutes a science and its objects. (p. 83)

We must not appropriate those whom we would try to know and understand by "colonizing" their experiences, by interpreting them from the perspective of the privileged expert (Opie, 1992). We must enter into a collaborative search for meaning with our clients and listen to their voices, their narratives, and their constructions of reality. It is significant that studies grounded in the subject's experience, that speak in the voices of oppressed people, and that promote the insurrection of subjugated knowledge have become classics. They are so immediate, so alive, and they teach us so much. Meyerhoff's *Number Our Days* (1978), Liebow's *Tally's Corner* (1968), Erikson's *Everything in Its Path* (1978), and Stack's *All Our Kin* (1974) are such works.

Recently in our own social work literature, Williams (1991) published a volume on black teenage mothers that brings to us their own perspectives, their own experiences, and their own words and presents a very different kind of picture than the large-scale epidemiological studies.

It is really not so complicated; we must ask people and then listen. And as we listen, we must attend to difference, to particularity, the contradictory, the paradoxical. As we do this, we will attend to that which may be quantifiably insignificant but whose presence may question a more conventional interpretation and expand understanding (Opie, 1992). Epidemiological studies are useful and important, but direct practice must be built on local knowledge, on the particular, on attention to difference and, most vital, on multiple voices. The questions to be asked and the interpretations of the data must be developed in collaboration between the researcher or practitioner and the one to be understood who is, after all, the expert. Knowledge and power are one, and when clients and subjects are collaborators in the discovery process, if their expertise is valued and affirmed, they are empowered.

This issue of *Social Work* [November 1992] seems at first to contain a range of somewhat unrelated articles about women, racism, academia, research, and people of color. But if we listen to Foucault, if we agree with him that knowledge is power and power is knowledge, we recognize the deep connection between the empowerment of oppressed people and the development and distribution of knowledge.

There is a painful paradox in being a professional and being committed to empowerment. A key part of the definition of a profession is the possession of knowledge and, in fact, the ownership of a specific area of knowledge. As professionals we are supposed to be experts, but the power in our expertise can disempower our clients and thus subvert the goals of our profession.

How can we resolve this paradox? Must we discard our knowledge, our accumulated professional wisdom? This would leave us adrift without anchor or compass. We need not discard our knowledge, but we must be open to local knowledge, to the narratives and truths of our clients. We must participate with them in the insurrection of subjugated knowledge. We must listen to honor and validate our client's expertise. We must learn to bracket our knowledge, to put it aside so it will not shape our questions and our listening and cause a barrier between us and the people we would understand. Furthermore, we must not privilege our professional knowledge, and we must let ourselves hear information from our clients that would challenge our views. We must attend. We have been mistaken before and we will be mistaken again. But we are only wrong when we continue to cling to our mistaken truths.

REFERENCES

American Psychiatric Association. (1980). *Diagnostic and statistical manual of mental disorders* (3rd ed.). Washington, DC: Author.
Baraka, I.A. (1971). Numbers, letters. In D. Randall (Ed.), *The black poets* (p. 218). New York: Bantam Books.
Collins, P.H. (1990). *Black feminist thought: Knowledge, consciousness, and the politics of empowerment.* New York: Unwin Hyman.
Erikson, K. (1978). *Everything in its path: Destruction of community in the Buffalo Creek Flood.* New York: Simon & Schuster.
Foucault, M. (1980). *Power/knowledge: Selected interviews and other writings.* New York: Pantheon Press.
Liebow, E., (1968). *Tally's corner.* Boston: Little Brown.
Meyerhoff, B. (1978). *Number our days.* New York: E.P. Dutton.
Opie, A. (1992, Spring). Qualitative research appropriation of the "other" and empowerment. *Feminist Review, 40,* 52-69.
Parker, I. (1989). Discourse and power. In J. Shotter & K.J. Gergen (Eds.), *Texts of identity* (pp. 56-69). London: Sage Publications.
Stack, C.B. (1974). *All our kin: Strategies for survival in a black community.* New York: Harper & Row.
White, M. & Epston, D. (1990). *Narrative means to therapeutic ends.* New York: W.W. Norton.
Williams, C.W. (1991). *Black teenage mothers: Pregnancy and child rearing from their perspectives.* Lexington, MA: Lexington Books. First published November 1992.

Listening to the Voices of Anorexia: The Researcher as an "Outsider-Witness"

Mary E. Olson

SUMMARY. This paper is based on a collaborative research inquiry with women who were formerly anorectic. Drawing on histories of female fasting, feminist cultural criticism, and women's psychology, the study examines the themes of voice and communication and develops relational research practices that allow a person to experience herself as whole. Reflexive and narrative ideas and conversational practices from family therapy are incorporated into an intensive case study method. Since the research proved beneficial to the participants, it may have important implications for more effective forms of therapy. *[Article copies available for a fee from The Haworth Document Delivery Service: 1-800-342-9678. E-mail address: <getinfo@haworthpressinc.com> Website: <http://www.haworthpressinc.com>]*

KEYWORDS. Anorexia, narrative therapy, female fasting, communication, voice, body

Biologically, physiologically, we are not so different from each other: historically, as narratives–we are each of us unique.

–Oliver Sacks, 1987, p. 111

Mary E. Olson, PhD, LICSW, is Adjunct Professor, Smith College School for Social Work, and a Research Fellow at its Center for Innovative Practice. She has a private practice in Northampton, MA.

Address correspondence to: Mary E. Olson, 151 Main Street, Northampton, MA 01060.

[Haworth co-indexing entry note]: "Listening to the Voices of Anorexia: The Researcher as an 'Outsider-Witness'." Olson, Mary, E. Co published simultaneously in *Journal of Feminist Family Therapy* (The Haworth Press, Inc.) Vol. 11, No. 4, 2000, pp. 25-46; and: *Feminism, Community, and Communication* (ed: Mary E. Olson) The Haworth Press, Inc., 2000, pp. 25-46. Single or multiple copies of this article are available for a fee from The Haworth Document Delivery Service [1-800-342-9678, 9:00 a.m. - 5:00 p.m. (EST). E-mail address: getinfo@haworthpressinc.com].

© 2000 by The Haworth Press, Inc. All rights reserved.

INTRODUCTION

This article describes the research I have been doing with women who have recovered from anorexia (Olson, 1999). My purpose has been to hear and record what the women have to say about their experiences of self-starvation. The study draws on a communication framework (Carey, 1988; Cronen, Johnson, & Lannamann, 1982; Geertz, 1983; Pearce & Cronen, 1980). Its focus includes the phenomenological meanings embodied by self-starvation and the way each woman used fasting to communicate about things felt to be unspeakable. Reflexive and narrative ideas and conversational practices from family therapy have been central to creating a research approach that evokes the imagination, creates joint authorship, and constitutes the women as subjects, rather than objects of expert scrutiny.

All of the major clinical writers on anorexia–Bruch (1978), Minuchin (1978), and Selvini-Palazzoli (1974; Selvini-Palazzoli & Viaro, 1988)–independently express the perception that anorectic girls and women need to experience themselves as whole, connected, and self-directed–as living selves, as subjects–rather than as blank, hollow, and skeletal patients. For this reason among others, I chose an intensive interview/case study method in order to hear what the women have to say within their own frames of reference, especially regarding topics that they may find difficult to express.

This qualitative approach, which fosters the voices of the participants, has become common in feminist and interpretive research of the last two decades (Belenky, Clinchy, Goldberger, & Tarule, 1986; Brown & Gilligan, 1992; Christians & Carey, 1981; Leeds-Hurwitz, 1995; Mishler, 1986). I further elaborated this method by writing the histories as complete narratives and asking the participants to read, edit, and comment on them. This method is an adaptation of Michael White's (1995a) concept of a "document of identity." In this essay, I will provide an example of one of these documents and illustrate how this communication research combines a form of inquiry about voice with relational research practices that can allow the person to experience herself as a living, vocal self.

THE RESEARCH QUESTIONS

What do women who actually have suffered from anorexia tell us about the meanings of food and body as signs and symbols, the communicative functions of self-starvation, and its contexts and purposes? Do cultural gender scripts of self-silencing and self-sacrifice influence the development of this symptom? These research questions come from the literature where I traced the themes of voice and communication within recent histories of female fasting and of anorexia, feminist cultural criticism, postmodern family therapy, and women's psychology.

THE HISTORY OF FEMALE FASTING

There have been two periods in Western history when fasting has been an important food practice among women. It occurred in Catholicism from the thirteenth to the sixteenth centuries in Europe, and during the nineteenth century, in Victorian society, when the first cases of secular fasting among young women appeared. Historians show that female self-starvation, for distinct reasons, occurred logically within each cultural system (Brumberg, 1988; Bynum, 1987).

Within medieval Catholicism, Caroline Walker Bynum (1987) observes that fasting was part of a female religious subculture, which emerged from lay communities. Such asceticism allowed religious women to acquire voice and to shape their positions within family, community, and institutional life.

As Bynum (1987) argues, the kitchen was territory controlled by women, thus making food a resource that women could access and use, pragmatically and symbolically, through its renunciation. On a practical, social level, refusing to eat became an effective way to control social circumstances and domestic pressures in the medieval family. Bodily functions, sexuality, fertility (menstruation), family members, religious superiors, and even God were susceptible to the influences of fasting. Some women thus managed to avoid medieval marriage, which often was brutal, and childbirth, which often was life threatening. The saint, Catherine of Siena (d. 1380), as an adolescent, starved herself, cut her hair, refused to sleep, and scalded her body in hot baths in order to avoid being married off by her family. Other religious women escaped the domestic role and converted husbands and fathers to their values of chastity and service by refusing to eat, doing charitable acts, and engaging in ecstatic trances.

On the spiritual level, women's fasting acted as an ingredient of female sanctity and part of the religious trajectory. According to Bynum, starvation was a way to fuse with a Christ whose suffering gave birth to the eternal life. In an era where Christ's humanity became the broken, bleeding flesh that fed the world, religious women saw Christ as female and their own ascetic suffering as *"imitatio Christi."*

Further, purgation through fasting, self-flagellation, and vigils was the basis of mystical experience that gave women legitimate claim to spiritual authority, in the absence of the formal education possessed by male priests. Extravagant female fasting occurred at a time when the Church was beginning to include women in its ranks, but in an emphatically second-class status. Female mysticism was the charismatic alternative to, and critique of, the masculine ecclesiastical hierarchy and the power of office. It was a transcendence of the second-rate place the Church was assigning women. As successful mystics, women were honored and respected. Their stature exempted them from the conventional restraints against women. Such women became leaders, teachers, writers, and reformers; thus, becoming full-fledged participants in a public life previously closed to them.

Spanning centuries and under a vastly different cultural system, privileged Victorian girls and women used food denial to signify social class, sexual purity, and spiritual worth. In an era of enormous sociological transition where an industrial masculine elite was forming, the women of the new upper ranks became the guardians of values, living symbols of purity, and ornamental reflections of male achievement within the separate and morally elevated domestic sphere (Douglas, 1977). Food practices and body image became central to the way that the Victorian lady distinguished herself from her heartier, working-class sisters. A delicate appetite was a sign of gentility and spirituality. Wasting was in vogue; debility was "positively fashionable" (Wood, 1973). In this way, female appetite signified multiple meanings about female identity. Joan Jacob Brumberg (1988, chap. 7) chronicles this important theme of "appetite as voice" and shows food and female body were "encoded" with complex social messages about character, morality, and class and comprised a "method of social stratification."

Given this cultural system, it is no wonder that Victorian adolescent girls learned to use appetite as a form of identity and self-expression. At the same time, the institution of the family was undergoing changes that shifted the meaning of food within the parent-child relationship. Food became love (Lasègue, 1873/Brumberg, 1988). In the Victorian world, eating became both an expression of female identity and a symbol of family relations and intergenerational reciprocity. Food practices that signaled proper female decorum at the dinner table easily turned into an instrument of emotional communication. Drawing on the writing of the nineteenth-century French physician, Charles Lasègue, Brumberg (1988) suggests that, within this era of repression, fasting served as a form of communication about otherwise forbidden or disqualified emotions. When goodwill between parents and daughter was jeopardized, for instance, fasting was the most effective means of communicating anger not only by interfering with dinner, but with the all-important, socially advantageous marriage.

In this way, Brumberg (1988) sketches the cultural and social antecedents for the emergence of anorexia nervosa in the late nineteenth century. She also describes the medicalization of female self-starvation. During the Victorian era, the cultural meaning of female fasting changed from a sign of piety to a sign of illness. The medicalization of anorexia occurred as part of a larger, epochal war between religion and science for power and dominance.

Women's illnesses provided an important battleground at a time when women were disestablished as healers and midwives, and male experts launched careers by exerting authority and colonizing previously female occupations, such as caring for the sick and tending women in childbirth (Douglas,1977; Ehrenreich & English, 1978). Obviously, the scientific position won in the battle over the definition of anorexia. Yet there was no actual explanation or theory behind this medical definition. Rather, it came from a descriptive orientation based on the diagnostic classification of diseases that had powerful political and economic agendas. The medicalization of anorexia bluntly obscured what Brumberg (1988) calls "the long tradition of girls and women who have used food and body as the focus of symbolic language (p. 46)."[1]

In sum, the work of historians direct us toward explanations that connect female fasting to the social world and cultural framework. Despite the vast differences between medieval Catholicism and Victorian times, there is a broad relationship, in each era, between the unsettled position of women, the links the culture made between women, food, and flesh, and fasting as embodied communication and a form of subjectivity. By subjectivity, I mean the capacity to influence one's identity and destiny, which converges with the idea of having a voice. These ideas resonate with our current world. Echoing these historians, we can ask how does a daughter use the practice of self-starvation as a voice in communicating about self and identity, shaping experience, and defining her place in family and community?

It must be kept in mind, however, that, in the medieval and Victorian periods, and even today, the fasting behavior of women was and is of interest to the society around them. There may have been other times and places–when such themes did not apply–that women starved themselves, but we do not know about it because no one, at the time, paid attention.

THE CONTEMPORARY PROBLEM

It is widely accepted that there is a cultural setting for anorexia nervosa in today's society. Since the 1960s, female fasting has been on the rise in the postindustrial world and has coincided with the glamorization of thinness. (Brumberg, 1988). While a traditional conception of femininity links women to food and body, modern Western culture currently idealizes female thinness, or women's transcendence of food, body, and even gender. This slenderness ideal has coincided with profound shifts and instabilities in gender relations brought on by reproductive freedom, the changes in sexual mores, the prevalence of divorce, and the women's movement, where unprecedented numbers of women have entered the workforce (Bordo, 1993; Brumberg, 1988). Cross-cultural research shows that while female self-starvation does exist outside the postindustrial world, eating disorders are prevalent only in contemporary societies influenced by thinness (Iancu, Spivak, Ratzoni, Apter, 1994).

The modern aesthetic of thinness is thus an important context for understanding anorexia. Feminist cultural critics–Kim Chernin (1981, 1985), Susie Orbach (1986), and Susan Bordo (1993)–argue that this aesthetic is a political, not just an arbitrary, fashion style. These thinkers interpret the slenderness ideal as a mystified form of social control. They observe that as women's presence in the public arena has increased, shedding flesh and its associations with the traditional female role has become a culturally endorsed approach to power, control, and success. Media imagery associated with the fashion industry and the beauty culture identifies the female self with the body, and the thin body with goodness, privilege, beauty, health, and worth. For Chernin, Orbach, and Bordo, thinness appears to signify a progressive narrative of female mastery, competence, and upward mobility, while it enforces a traditional pattern of female self-denial and self-censorship.

This cultural perspective also defines anorexia as a form of language and communication. Orbach and Bordo both propose that girls and women who starve themselves appropriate this public vocabulary of thinness and use it to communicate and shape experience in a multiplicity of idiosyncratic ways. While these authors acknowledge that anorexia is undesirable and harmful, they also see that the symptom has meaning. Orbach (1986) writes that anorexia is "an [understudy] of the unspeakable" (p. 24), while Bordo (1993) says that anorexia is an attempt to create an honorable identity "with the vocabulary and the syntax of the body, like those of all languages, culturally given" (p. 67).

At the same time, there are questions about anorexia nervosa that the cultural model cannot answer. While anorexia derives from the language of thinness, people mediate the culture and use its symbols in complex and particular ways within the context of an immediate social world. Postmodern family therapists offer a paradigm that sheds light on social processes in a way that is consistent with an emphasis on voice and communication.

In this regard, I owe an enormous debt to the book, *The Body Speaks* (1994), written by James and Melissa Griffith. Although these authors do not address the specific problem of anorexia, they show that a non-organic, mind-body symptom points to the presence of an "unspeakable dilemma," or double bind as conceptualized by Gregory Bateson (1962; Bateson, Jackson, Haley, Weakland, 1956). It is, in its simplest form, a silencing of the self in order to protect a vital relationship.

> "Having a voice" seems to be a code phrase for "expressing who I know myself to be." As discussed, many mind-body symptoms arise out of dilemmas of expression–*if I show myself as I know myself then I fear I will no longer fit within this relationship I must preserve. I risk*

losing either the relationship or my sense of selfhood. I may be spewed out; I may look in the mirror but see no one. Mind-body problems are a performance of this dilemma. [Italics added.] (Griffith & Griffith, 1994, p. 63)

In such a situation, a person might try to sustain the relationship by suppressing her voice and body. Yet, the body (emotions, hunger) does not cooperate fully with such intentions and instead expresses metaphorically the person's dilemma in the mutated form of mind-body symptom. Like escaping one's own shadow, self-silencing is never totally possible. Regarding anorexia, I began to see that self-starvation may draw on the language of food and body with the intention of resolving feelings of unacceptability and become instead the body's "performance of the unspeakable." The Griffiths' concept of an unspeakable dilemma gave me a new way to start listening to the stories of anorectics.

To add yet another layer of complexity, I began to see that this double-bind description tends to capture more than just the individual situation. Double-bind communication seems to be built into the social experience of girls growing up in our society. Research into women's psychology points to patterns of gender socialization that encourage self-silencing in the name of connection and thus produce the experience of unspeakable dilemmas. As Lyn Brown and Carol Gilligan (1992) show, our culture invites the silencing of the female voice and body by promoting "the tyranny of the nice and kind" and the "power of the perfect." Feminine ideals prescribe an image of feminine perfection that encourages complex, "unfeminine," emotional experiences and hungers to be suppressed. Brown and Gilligan call this "a relational paradox"–"the giving up of relationships for the sake of Relationships." Similarly, Jean Baker Miller and Irene Pierce Stiver (1997) see "strategies of disconnection"–variations of self-silencing in order to protect the self and essential relationships–as being at the heart of female psychological problems.

Most girls and women navigate these cultural minefields without developing a self-destructive, life-threatening eating problem. While cultural ideals and gender prescriptions set the stage, there must be a personal context that sets the final result in motion. More precisely, at various levels of context–e.g., family, peer group, and culture–there may be multiple, unspeakable dilemmas involved in a mind-body problem, which, in a complex way, conveys what the person cannot say with words. By chronicling the testimonies of women who have had anorexia, the study illuminates this hazily lit corner of the culture where definitions of femininity converge and interact with human suffering.

Drawing on John Shotter (1984), my purpose was to see whether the idea of anorexia as symbolic, embodied communication found a fit with the women's narratives in my study, rather than to think I could discover objective truths that were separate from my stance as a researcher. In each case, as I try to show, there was a strong resonance between the ideas informing the research and the stories of the women, who also were asked to read the written narratives and comment on them. The question is whether this perspective is helpful, compassionate, and emancipatory, rather than whether it is right in any absolute sense.

THE INTERVIEWS

In the initial study, I interviewed four women who had been anorectic and recovered.[2] At the outset, I explained to each woman the purpose of the interviews: "I am basically interested in hearing your story and having a conversation with you about how you understand anorexia. There are many things professionals do not know about anorexia, and we need the knowledge that you have of it. My hope is to learn from people who had been through it and recovered, so we might provide more effective help to other people with this illness." All the participants appreciated the rationale and expressed a positive feeling about being able to contribute to this project, especially if it could help someone.

Many of the interview questions came from the family-therapy literature and were designed not only to elicit a life history but also to engage the participants' imaginations and capacities for meaning making (Griffith & Griffith, 1994; Imber-Black, Roberts & Whiting, 1988; Steiner-Adair, 1990; Sheinberg & Penn, 1991; White, 1990).[3] The topics included the person's history of anorexia, family (including food practices and dinner scenes), recovery, experience of the body, and gender premises. While I attempted to follow the semi-structured interview schedule, I also changed the order in which the questions were raised based on the natural flow of the conversation. The interviews were also structured by the participants who offered a wealth of observations and details about which I never would have thought to ask.

As much as possible, I conducted the interviews using a reflective style and active listening. My stance was speculative and exploratory and made room for the voice of the participants. I listened to the language and explored the experiences of the women interviewed. I tried to make the interviews conversations. This aim was influenced by research in women's psychology that shows that women's voices tend to emerge most clearly from processes of collaboration (Belenky et al., 1986). At the same time, where I included questions about voice, silence, and communication, my perspective shaped the interviews. I pursued these themes through direct questions such as: "Do you think anorexia is connected with a struggle to have a voice? If so, what do you think you were trying to communicate?" There were also reflexive questions such as: "What did food and body mean in your family growing up? Do you think they were symbols of anything?" I was careful to establish a climate of safety and check in with the participants about how they were feeling during the interviews. These questions about the immediate comfort level produced rich emotional information, but none of the participants ever wanted to stop.

DOCUMENTS OF IDENTITY

Michael White's term, *documents of identity*, refers to a variety of counter-cultural practices that make otherwise marginalized and invisible people active participants in constructing and authenticating their own histories. Borrowing from the cultural anthropologist, Barbara Myerhoff, White emphasizes the role of the "outsider-witness" who plays a critical role in the acknowledgement of a person's worth and vitality, while authenticating their claims about their histories and identities. While White develops the therapeutic implications of these concepts, such ideas also have important significance for doing research, especially with anorectic women for whom the themes of marginality and invisibility are quite salient. While I did not follow White's technique of externalizing conversation, I took several important ideas from his work. Instead of viewing myself as a neutral researcher, my role became closer to that of an outsider-witness, since the research promoted "reflexive self-consciousness" and enabled the "interviewee's participation in the authorship of her own life" (White, 1995b, p. 178). The study thus defined the participants as "storytellers in a narrative context," rather than respondents in a survey context (Barbetta, 1991). The practical steps involved in co-authoring the document of identity were simple. In writing the narratives, I tried to stay as close to the participants' words and meanings as possible and then, I asked them to read and rewrite their stories. The participants had veto power and narrative control. Any changes made to the narratives were based on the responses of the participants.

The following is a document of identity that came from the study. I first met Nell, an editor whose name has been changed, when I asked her to do some editing. In the course of our conversation, she learned about my research interest and volunteered to participate in the study. After the initial study, when I met with her several times, I again interviewed her in order to clarify further what she had meant by "the Kirk curse" and to follow up her experience in being part of the research. Nell told me that the study helped her put the past in perspective and reminded her of her "strength and wisdom," thus encouraging her to focus on what she now wanted to do with her life. She has read and endorsed the following narrative.

THE KIRK CURSE

Nell Kirk is a 52-year-old copy editor from a Yankee family that she describes as "doomed and suffering from a curse." Yet, at this point in her life, Nell is happily married to her second husband, has a 27-year-old son from her first marriage, and a 2-year-old granddaughter. Nell works for a newspaper and does free-lance editing on the side. When describing her occupation as an editor, she says good-naturedly that her business is "correcting other people's mistakes." Warm, kind-hearted, and very intelligent, Nell talks openly about her experience of anorexia and of a troubled earlier life.

What quickly becomes apparent is that there are different chapters in Nell's life with different identities: the highly successful college graduate; the thirty-something waitress, who worked at a diner and was a survivor of the sixties and seventies counterculture; and the gracious, youthful woman I now encounter. You might not guess meeting Nell that she went to a prestigious college, so much has the course of her life worn away any obvious signs of privilege. Once you begin listening carefully to her, however, you notice that her observations illuminate in a rare way, and her language is literate, beautiful, with traces of metaphors and occasional pieces of poetry.

Nell's anorexia occurred (atypically) when Nell was 35 years old and lasted for two years. The precipitating events were the death of her mother and returning home to live with her father. During this time, Nell's weight dropped from 130 lbs. to 99 lbs. at 5'4". Her periods stopped. (She experienced their absence as "liberating.") When I interviewed her at the present time, she appeared thin at her current weight of 120 lbs. She showed me a picture of herself when she was anorectic and looked, in her words, "haunted and emaciated." There is a dense context surrounding the anorexia. Her anorexia had complex emotional and psychological roots in her childhood and upbringing and was part of a much larger story of her struggle for self, voice, and agency.

The Family Story

Nell is the oldest child and only daughter of three children born to a newspaper journalist and his wife who worked as a statistician. Both parents were alcoholics. Their marriage was difficult and conflict-ridden. While Nell was growing up, her father had affairs. Nell's mother became "heavy and sick" and the recipient of emotional and physical abuse by the father. Childhood was, for Nell, a time that felt chaotic and violating. She was a "chubby" youngster and adolescent, using food as a source of comfort. Nell's school successes brought honor to her family and herself while she carefully shielded her family and herself from exposure and shame. She was aware of what other people might think of her parents, especially her mother. Nell had friends, but never invited them to her house. Until high school, she confided in no one about the situation at home. She knew how her parents would look to the world and maintained a code of protection.

Dinnertime was a symbolic battleground for the parents' relationship. These scenes were filled with conflict because the whole process of making dinner was a daily struggle. Despite the fact that both parents drank after work, the mother's performance seemed be what was at stake here, and thus, the source of contention. For Nell, food and eating came to represent a "constant battle between good and evil." To this day, food has remained a symbol of conflict between her "great interest in food" and her great capacity for self-denial.

Despite these difficulties, Nell knew that her parents loved her. Her mother was the source of "unconditional love"; while her father's love felt more complicated and prized. Each parent competed for her affection, although when her mother was drinking, she found ways to retaliate against Nell for her relationship with her father. Nell admired her father, who encouraged his academically gifted daughter to excel, which she did. As an editor, her father always was "correcting [her] mistakes" in academic assignments when Nell preferred her work to be her own. ("I wanted it to be mine.") There was an early struggle in Nell's relationship with her father to have her own voice, without his editorial interference. At the same time, Nell was in a privileged position with her father, since he treated his daughter better and seemed to value her more than he did his wife. Her father positioned his daughter to be a rival to her mother and thus generated a triangle producing psychological dilemmas and loyalty conflicts that reached far into Nell's adult life. This family story of a dominant father, a devalued mother, and a chosen daughter helps explain the issues Nell seems to have had in the genesis of the anorexia.

The Illness

Nell's mother died of an alcohol-related illness in the fall of 1981. She was ill for weeks before her death. Nell's father had Korsakov's syndrome, a memory disorder, by the time of the mother's death. For this reason, it did not occur to her father to notify the children. Nell learned of her death three days after it happened. Nell's mother was her father's conservator and, as executor of her estate, Nell had to apply to succeed her as conservator.

When asked how she accounted for the onset of anorexia, Nell replied: "Guilt over the death of my mother." Shortly after her death, Nell returned to live with her father in the house where she grew up. She recalled a conversation she had with Fred, who is now her husband, telling him, "I have to go there." She added in her interview with me: "Louisa May Alcott raised me. She was my moral preceptor. Moral codes were in books. . . . I grew up in a vacuum. Except politically. My parents were strong, moral Democrats." In this way, Nell conveyed that she felt the kind of obligation to take care of her father that was closer to the worldview and the moral order of a century ago. Nell subscribed to a nineteenth-century code of care and duty in a culture and society for whom that has little meaning.

In retrospect, Nell's decision to go home evoked a variety of different insights. She was searching for a purpose in her life, and this gave her one. Prior to this period, Nell saw herself as in danger of becoming an alcoholic and was frightened about heading for a "dead-end" life like her alcoholic mother. For five years in the late seventies, Nell and Fred were both drinking and generally spent the summers camping and traveling. At the time of her mother's death, neither Nell nor her husband had a job and they were living "a hand-to-mouth existence." So, taking care of her father was a job that Nell needed and really wanted. She fought with her brothers about who would be responsible for him. Someone had to be there, because he was capable of setting the house on fire and could not take care of his daily needs or pay his bills. Nell also observed that by going home she was reliving her adolescence and, this time, "would make it work." She wanted to rewrite the past and its legacy.

The Return to Father

Her father had developed Korsakov's syndrome as a result of heavy drinking. Korsakov's is a form of memory loss due to neuron degeneration from alcohol. Oliver Sacks' (1987) brilliant portrait of "The Lost Mariner" is a description of a middle-aged man with a severe and devastating form of Korsakov's. Sacks renders the tragic existential situation of a person who is "dissolving" due to severe memory lapses about recent events, yet who may well have recollections from long ago. Without memory or continuity, the person with Korsakov's suffers "radical lostness," "without roots, or rooted only in the remote past" (p. 29). Sacks describes how such people live in a "time capsule," sealed off from an actual and coherent experience of the present, which leaves only brief, fleeting, isolated impressions.

Nell's father was in his own time capsule, which Nell joined for a period. In listening to her, I first was struck by the ways she had mirrored her father's despair. Nell returned home, because she, too, felt lost in a profound, existential sense. Her anorexia let her waste away, much as her father was disintegrating from abusing alcohol and his body. Each living in the past, father and daughter were both present, yet absent, dissolving, as it were, from Korsakov's and anorexia, respectively. The dead mother, who had destroyed herself by drinking with her husband and not setting any limits, had literally been lost, although she retained a powerful presence in death. This strange feeling of radical lostness–of being there, yet not–ran through this family at this moment in their history.

In other words, Nell was living with her parents' ghosts and fending off a feeling of dissolution. When asked what specific emotions were connected to the practice of self-starvation, Nell replied, "Fear of loss, of rejection, of sinking into the abyss, and most of all, turning out like my parents." Not eating and running provided experiences of "joyous affirmation." Paradoxically, in her mind, these practices counteracted the threat of nonexistence.

For the first year with her father, Nell spent her time "cleaning up the mess." Her parents' home was a beautiful place that had been neglected and run down. Nell stayed up till the wee hours of the morning polishing fixtures that had not been cleaned in years. On the surface, Nell was helping her father get the house ready to be sold. Her parents had a huge amount of debt. They had been spending their days drinking vodka and had not worked for several years. The only way to cover the debt they had incurred was by selling the house. The meaning of this year, however, carried a deeper significance. The themes of cleaning and creating order seemed to be linked to feelings of ascetic purification and spiritual redemption, both of the self and of the family as a whole. Nell stopped drinking at this point, and, in her mind, began saving her life.

Nell linked the anorexia to the larger project of creating order and gaining control over her circumstances and other people, especially her father. She said, with a degree of self-derision, that she thought that she would be able to set things right and make a new life with her father. She hoped to create the idealized relationship she thought possible with him, based on her privileged position as a child. That this hope was disappointed seemed evident in her remarks. Nevertheless, at the time, Nell believed that by fasting and becoming thin she was able to influence her father, who had abused her heavy mother, and protect herself from similar violation and mistreatment. She said, "If I am thin, I am immune from his despising me." His approval was garnered by thinness; the self-denial also mitigated her sense of guilt toward her mother. In the process, Nell established her own sense of agency and self-determination. Self-starvation gave her the voice she had always struggled to have with her father, while ensuring her acceptability and her dominance: "I'm in control; you can no longer control me."

Abstaining from food, which was a symbol of her mother, became a way of also controlling herself. For Nell, this symbolic use of food was interwoven with the symbolic meaning of the body. The fat body connoted the passivity and vulnerability of her mother, who had become an abused victim of life, especially the circumstances in her marriage. Nell rebelled against the mother's destiny by gaining control of what she saw as her own excesses, food and alcohol. By becoming emaciated, she attempted to please and exert leverage over her father, to save and to protect herself from a "dead-end" life, and yet to register the profound impact of her mother's tragedy. Ultimately, she gave her mother's death meaning by making it an occasion of a physical, spiritual, and psychic regeneration.

Mother's Ghost

Nell's complicated feelings about her mother created a powerful impetus for her fasting behavior. There had been an edge of competition between them that could not be communicated directly, because of Nell's desire to protect her mother. Nell was expressing it instead in the way she took care of the house and her own body: "I can do this better than you do. The house will be clean. Everything will be orderly." She was trying to show something to her mother about "how to fix it," meaning how to fix the situation in the family.

Yet, this whole project eventually turned into a kind of suicidal competition. The competition coexisted with intense guilt and loss. Nell felt that she had somehow wronged her mother, especially by not being there when she died. Cadaverous thinness was a way to declare her allegiance to her dead mother by resembling "death warmed over." Finally, the self-starvation removed whatever incestuous taint Nell might have felt in stepping into her mother's role vis-à-vis her father. The only way to be close to her father was to be extremely thin and without sexual characteristics.

Yet, even in competing with her mother, Nell was loyal to her. Even though she was quite angry at her mother for "not shaping up," she also identified with her. Ultimately, Nell wished that her mother had been strong enough to stand up to and leave her husband. Nell's self-starvation expressed her own need for penance and absolution, while her self-control and extreme jogging expressed her anger and her refusal to be likewise doomed.

Nell agreed when I asked whether she poured paradoxical meanings into her anorexia. It was a way of dying and of recreating the self–a mixture of self-sacrifice and self-renewal; service to others and self-definition. There was no dualism here. Complicated emotional experiences were expressed and united through the body.

Unspeakable Dilemmas

Nell and I explored the question of why the body became the site of such a struggle. We agreed on several conclusions, based on what I already have said about the symbolic meanings of food and body. First, Nell was trying to work out her own issues of self, voice, and agency in the context of her relationships with two parents, with whom there could be no conversation.

The father had Korsakov's; the mother was dead. Therefore, if Nell was to communicate with her father and mother, she needed to find a different language. Nell's father failed to recall what she said and was unable to retain the present, so words and dialogue carried little possibility for emotional exchange. In addition, her father was an editor and previously had colonized language. Words could be edited, while the analogic communication using her body could not be disqualified. As far as communicating with her mother went, Nell thought that she was using self-starvation to speak to her in a way that was hard perhaps for others to hear.

Nell could not leave her mother or her father in a psychological sense as long as guilt, obligation, and negative identification tied her to them. The Milan Associates (Boscolo, Cecchin, Hoffman, and Penn, 1987) say that people cannot leave home under a negative connotation. At the same time, there was no obvious solution to this dilemma, and it was not possible to have the kind of conversation and reflection that might produce one (Griffith & Griffith, 1994). Not eating substituted as a form of voice about life-important issues in the absence of verbal communication and real emotional exchange. While the anorexia ultimately was endangering, it was also a product of the way that Nell was trying to generate new possibilities for her family and herself.

Our final conclusion as to why the body became the site of this struggle was that self-starvation was consistent with how society has invited women to be. To this observation, Nell added, "It was also the eighties when everybody was getting rich." In the affluent community where Nell lived with her father, she also worked for several families as a child-care person to make extra money. She remembered feeling that in the face of the wealth and position of the women in these families, she at least had "being thin." Thinness was an accomplishment that she could show the world. It was a way of belonging to a society that she felt she could not fit into in other ways. For instance, Nell said they didn't have the money to go shopping; they were just managing to survive. Being thin in a place where "you can't be too thin or too rich" bestowed prestige.

The Recovery

Interestingly, Nell's recovery began when she formed a friendship with one of the women she worked for, and found to be quite different from the other rich women in that town. Her friend had been a struggling artist before her marriage and began showing concern for Nell, which helped her shift away from her extreme, anorectic stance. For instance, Nell joined her friend's aerobics class rather than running miles every day by herself. This friendship signaled Nell's beginning distance from her father and was one of several relationships that were crucial in fostering her recovery. Nell's best friend from college told her she was anorectic, as did another close friend. Their concern and feedback began to break the spell of the anorexia, creating a bridge back to normal eating and social behavior. These friends were a circle of outsider-witnesses in Michael White's sense.

At the same time that Nell was connecting or reconnecting with women friends, she was coming to terms with what it meant to lose her mother and how much she had loved and missed her. It was quite moving to listen to Nell talk about this recognition and about the forgiveness it implied. She also began to realize that her father loved her mother: "He missed her. He never forgot she was dead, despite the Korsakov's, and was completely lost without her." Although Nell "sort of" knew that he loved her before, his intense response to her death registered this for her emotionally. The fact that her father finally acknowledged his love for her mother profoundly altered Nell's feelings about her, too.

This outcome may have saved Nell's life although it may, for a time, have contributed to the anorexia. To explain this further, the reigning myth, or story, in the family, while Nell was growing up, was that the father and daughter shared a special intellectual potential while the mother was holding them back. Father and daughter were the privileged, "competent" couple, and the mother was the "incompetent" one, as symbolized by her weight and domestic failures.

When Nell returned home, she hoped to activate the relationship with her father, which would be the springboard to a more successful life. During the first year when she became anorectic, she was struggling with the issue of being preferred by her father over her mother. There were various, long-standing expressions of conflict in the areas of food behavior, intellectual achievement, and body image. But in living with her father, Nell realized that her father's grief meant he had actually loved her mother, and she could not replace her. This knowledge weakened the old myth.

Consequently, Nell slowly began to recognize her own love for her mother. She went through her mother's old letters; and in that process began to trace her love for her mother and her mother' love for her. Now, instead of being a competitor, Nell began to develop a new narrative, which allowed her to experience herself as a daughter grieving her parent.

In addition, the debunking of the reigning family myth freed Nell to identify openly with her father and become an editor herself, without feeling disloyal to her mother. Before her mother's death, Nell had taken on her mother's ethic of self-sacrifice, but once the relational story had shifted, she could begin to shed this burden. Her economy of emotion was thus converted from scarcity, rivalry and guilt to compassion, forgiveness, and love.

Nell's relationship with Fred, her husband, and Julian, her 10-year-old son, also played a role in extracting her from this situation. Nell loved Fred dearly, but her relationship with him was in turmoil, because of her insistence on living with her father. In our interviews, she said that after about a year living with her father, she realized that she might lose Fred and did not want to risk this. She was quite worried about the impact of her absence on Julian, who was now staying with his father most of the time. Fred stayed with Nell when he could, but spent about half the time working in the same town as Julian. Julian did not want to leave his friends and school to be with Nell, so Fred and Julian would drive down and visit Nell on the weekends.

After about two years living with her father, Nell decided to take action and found a rest home for him. She moved him back to the town where Fred and Julian lived, and she and her brothers, who lived there too, sold the family's original house and paid off the debts. Nell got a job waitressing, eventually landing the job she now has with the newspaper. Her father died in 1993, but before that time Nell had helped him to stop drinking. His mental condition improved greatly in those latter years, and Nell and her brothers managed to see him virtually every day until his death.

In this way, rather than looking at the anorexia as an individual "disorder," Nell's story shows how female self-starvation can be viewed in its wider context as part of a symbolic system within the family and culture. Food is linked to the female role, and the female body is seen as an emblem of the self (Brumberg, 1988, 1997; Bynum, 1987). Nell's experiences within her family shaped her ideas of food and body that the wider culture then supported. The opposite also is true, that the wider culture formed the family's notions of food and body that then became interwoven with relational meanings, struggles, and dilemmas.

The Kirk Curse

But beyond these relational influences, there is also the mysterious curse Nell spoke of. She said it started as "a bitter jest" but spoke to something serious. Nell traced the curse to her father's sense of failure and his drinking. His real dream in life had been to be a great American writer, and his hero was Hemingway. As a young man, he had been a "bright light," but his writing career was ultimately not successful, which left him in despair. Nell said that the "family curse" was "a whole complex of things" that were associated with her father's literary temperament and tragic ambition. She suspected that it probably went back generations, although she was not sure how. It amounted to "the feeling that we were somehow negatively chosen–separate from the rest of the world and afflicted with things that other people weren't afflicted with." Nell talked about Laing's metaphor of "knots," premises that are passed from one generation to the next. In her family, there seemed to be this double legacy of ambition and the terrible paralysis that ensues from having to do something great.

She has felt her own life tied up with this knot and those of her two brothers. Her father had Nell slotted to become a scholar. Yet, his dream not only created divided loyalties for her, but gave her the feeling that she too was incapable of living up to family expectations, thus leading to the same sense of paralysis. For periods of time, each of her brothers also became immobilized and alcoholic. Only when "the curse" started to be resolved, was Nell able to abandon the symptoms afflicting her and pursue her own life. Her brothers' lives also have improved over the years. Gus, the youngest, who had stopped drinking before the mother's death, built a contracting business. Ted, who only recently became sober, now works as a caretaker in a residence for mentally ill adults. Nell still worries about Ted who continues to seem troubled by the past. She may show him this document of identity as an attempt to help him.

To summarize, at a critical juncture, Nell described the practice of self-starvation as an important voice for communicating about her identity and defining her place in family and community. Alternatives to this practice seemed unavailable to her in the face of the Kirk curse: her legacies of alcoholism and paralysis, her father's domination and debility, the tragic death of her mother and the inherent difficulty of speaking about complex emotional issues without risking further violation and loss. Self-silencing and self-sacrifice were thus important themes for Nell. Fasting and taking care of her father gave her a sense of self and agency in contrast to her fears of becoming invisible. Finally, the recovery from the anorexia started as a result of the meanings Nell took from her father's grief and from her mother's letters. In other words, new perceptions were produced that released Nell from the severity of her food practices and set her free.

As a final note, it is interesting to point out that the whole period with her father was a deliberate choice by Nell, rather than something imposed. She was not a victim. In fact, this episode in her life awakened her to her own capacity to act as a subject–that is, a person in control of her life and of her destiny.

I received the following letter from Nell when we completed her narrative:

> Mary:
>
> I read your account and analysis of a dark period in my life gratefully. You've shown me the strength and wisdom of my own psyche–a gift from myself that surprises me.
>
> I know I struggled out of that time with great relief–though the issue of control still manifests in how I view my body, and "thinness" is still a seductive goal. I think that's something that haunts former anorexics, perhaps American women in general.
>
> Certainly, I've freed myself to move into a more "successful" life–though perhaps because of a wholehearted acceptance of youthful

values, I still define success as "right livelihood" rather than in terms of today's culture.

Now I'm trying to redirect the energy I waste worrying about what I look like into more creative avenues.

Seeing my life through your lens has brought the picture into much sharper focus. Thank you for that.

"Nell"

CONCLUSION

My experience writing about the lives of these women has taken me into worlds of suffering that have mystery, beauty, depth, and strength. I tried to preserve the integrity of each story, rather than to use the more conventional forms of systematic analysis that render patterns and themes, but lose context and narrative structure. I thought that by writing *tales,* I might contribute to our understanding and to that of the person about whose life I am writing (Sacks, 1987).

Making the concept of embodied communication central to the idea of anorexia has proven clarifying and compassionate. The deconstruction of food and body as symbols has given access to the particular worlds of these women. There is imaginative power in exploring these meanings, not as theoretically derived, but as phenomenologically derived. They provide access to the person and to the social world in a way that renders a "thickness" of description and an entrance into the imaginative universe (Geertz, 1973).

Nell's story and her comments show the value of using this approach. The research method–adapted from Michael White's (1995a) documents of identity–also may have implications for doing therapy with anorexic girls and women when they are in the later, post-starvation phase. The jointly authored account offers a method of collaboration that provides an organizing and integrating narrative structure that lets the women experience themselves as whole. Bonds of connection formed between the women and me as I interviewed them, carefully attended to their meanings, and wrote about their lives. Quite unexpectedly, as a researcher, I seemed to form healing relationships with these women. The process of participating in this study has produced a new sense of possibility both for them and for me.

This project is ultimately about giving language to suffering. As Elaine Scarry (1985), who creates a complex, dense, and moral argument for the expression of physical pain, writes: "Physical suffering destroys language, and moral rightness (in the Old Testament as in most other human contexts) tends to lie with the most articulate" (p. 201). In *Wasted: A Memoir of*

Anorexia and Bulimia, Marya Hornbacher (1998), tells a harrowing story of fourteen years in "the netherworld" and comments about the absence of language during this time:

> It is impossible to sufficiently articulate an inarticulate process, a very wordless time. I did not learn to live by words, so I have found myself with few words to describe what happened . . . I have added words, color, and chronology to a time in my life that appears to me a pile of random frames scattered over the floor of my brain . . . I'm often surprised that I exist. (p. 279)

Girls and women who are engaged in self-starvation are threatened by invisibility and nonexistence. Finding a compassionate language for their experience can help them acquire a voice. Exploring what self-starvation means to them, and interpreting these meanings in psychological, social and cultural contexts, is a step toward agency. With these concerns in mind, this study has attempted to integrate communication and voice as significant themes both in the content of the narratives and in the form of the research. As the participants in the study found the process itself beneficial, I hope that it will have implications for more effective forms of therapy as well.

NOTES

1. There are, of course, severe medical consequences of starvation (Keys, Brozek, Henschel, Mickelsen & Taylor, 1950). Anorexia can become a medical condition, but it starts out with a deliberate decision to fast, which is an action that must be understood within its social context and cultural framework.

2. I located the participants in several, purposive ways and interviewed women with clinical and nonclinical histories. The women ranged in ages from 21 to 51 years old and were white and middle-class. Three were heterosexual; one woman was lesbian. The specific criteria for participation included weight gain, participation in school or work, and the development of meaningful relationships. Please see the complete dissertation (Olson, 1999) for a full description of the methods.

3. Please see Olson (1999) for the interview schedule.

The author wishes to express appreciation to Sally Friedman, Michael Morgan, and Elizabeth Petroff for their contributions to the research and to Carol Olson and Lynn Hoffman for their editorial suggestions.

REFERENCES

Barbetta, P. (1991). *Relational dilemmas in child care: Microanalysis of an Italian story.* Unpublished manuscript

Bateson, G. (1962). A note on the double bind. In C. Sluzki and D. Ransom (Eds.) (1976), *Double bind: The foundation of the communicational approach to the family* (pp.39-42). New York: Grune & Stratton

Bateson, G., Jackson, D., Haley, J., & Weakland, J. (1956). Toward a theory of schizophrenia. In C. Sluzki and D. Ransom (Eds.) (1976), *Double bind: The foundation of the communicational approach to the family* (pp.3-22). New York: Grune & Stratton

Belenky, M. F., Clinchy, B.M., Goldberger, N. R., & Tarule, J. M. (1986). *Women's ways of knowing. The development of self voice, and mind.* New York: Basic Books.

Bordo, S. (1993). *Unbearable weight: Feminism, western culture, and the body.* Berkeley and Los Angeles: University of California Press.

Boscolo, L., Cecchin, G., Hoffman, L., & Penn, P. (1987). *Milan systemic family therapy: Conversations in theory and practice.* New York: Basic Books.

Brown, L. M., & Gilligan, C. (1992). *Meeting at the crossroads.* Cambridge: Harvard University Press.

Bruch, H. (1978). *The golden cage: The enigma of anorexia nervosa.* Cambridge: Harvard University Press.

Brumberg, J. J. (1988). *Fasting girls: The history of anorexia nervosa.* Cambridge: Harvard University Press.

Brumberg, J. J. (1997). *The body project: An intimate history of American girls.* New York: Random House.

Bynum, C. W. (1987). *Holy feast and holy fast: The religious significance of food to medieval women.* Berkeley and Los Angeles: University of California Press.

Carey, J. W. (1988). *Communication as culture: Essays on media and society.* Boston: Unwin Hyman.

Chernin, K. (1981). *The obsession: Reflections of the tyranny of slenderness.* New York: Harper & Row.

Christians, C. G., & Carey, J. W. (1981). The logic and aims of qualitative research. In G. H. Stemple & B. H. Westley (Eds.), *Research methods in mass communication.* Englewood Cliffs: Prentice-Hall

Cronen, V. E., Johnson, K. M., & Lannamann, J.W. (1982). Paradoxes, double binds, and reflexive loops: An alternative theoretical perspective. *Family Process, 21,* 91-112

Douglas, A. (1977). *The feminization of American culture.* New York: Doubleday.

Ehrenreich, B., & English, D. (1978). *For her own good: 150 years of experts' advice to women.* New York: Doubleday.

Geertz, C. (1973). *The interpretation of cultures.* New York: Basic Books.

Geertz, C. (1983). *Local knowledge: Further essays in interpretive anthropology.* New York: Basic Books.

Gilligan, C. (1982). *In a different voice: Psychological theory and women's development.* Cambridge: Harvard University Press.

Griffith, J. L., & Griffith, M. E. (1994). *The body speaks: Therapeutic dialogues for mind-body problems.* New York: Basic Books

Hornbacher, M. (1998). *Wasted: A memoir of anorexia and bulimia.* New York: HarperPerennial.

Iancu, I., Spivak, B., Ratzoni, G., Apter, A. (1994). The sociocultural theory in the development of anorexia nervosa. *Psychopathology, 27,* 29-36.

Imber-Black, E., Roberts, J., & Whiting, R. (1988). *Rituals in families and family therapy.* New York and London: Norton.

Keys, A., Brozek, J., Henschel, A., Mickelsen, O., & Taylor, H. L. (1950). *The biology of human starvation* (2 vols.). Minneapolis: University of Minnesota Press.

Leeds-Hurwitz, W. (1995). *Social approaches to communication.* New York and London: Guilford.

Lasègue, C. "On Hysterical Anorexia," Medical Times and Gazette (September 6, 1873), pp. 256-266.

Miller, J. B. & Stiver, I. P. (1997) *The healing connection: How women form relationships in therapy and in life.* Boston: Beacon Press.

Minuchin, S., Rosman, B. L., & Baker, L. (1978). *Psychosomatic families: Anorexia nervosa in context.* Cambridge: Harvard University Press.

Mishler, E. (1986). *Research interviewing: Context and narrative.* Cambridge, MA: Harvard University Press.

Olson, M. (1999). *Voices of anorexia: A study of voice, communication, and the body.* Unpublished doctoral dissertation, University of Massachusetts, Amherst.

Orbach, S. (1986). *Hunger strike: The anorectic's struggle as a metaphor for our age.* New York: Norton.

Pearce, W. B. & Cronen, V. E. (1980). *Communication, action, and meaning: The creation of social realities.* New York: Praeger.

Sacks, O. (1987). *The man who mistook his wife for a hat and other clinical tales.* New York: Harper & Row.

Scarry, E. (1985). *The body in pain: The making and unmaking of the world.* New York and Oxford: Oxford University Press.

Selvini-Palazzoli, M. (1974). *Self-starvation* (A. Pomerans, Trans.). London: Chaucer. (original work published 1963).

Selvini-Palazzoli, M. & Viaro, M. (1988). The anorectic process in the family: A six-stage model as a guide for individual therapy. *Family Process, 27,* 129-148

Sheinberg, M. & Penn, P. (1991). Gender dilemmas, gender questions and the gender mantra. *Journal of Marital and Family Therapy, 17,* 33-44.

Shotter, J. (1984). *Social accountability and selfhood.* Oxford: Basil Blackwell.

Steiner-Adair, C. (1990). The body politic: Normal female adolescent development and the development of eating disorders. In C. Gilligan, N. P. Lyons, & T. J. Hanmer (Eds.), *Making Connections* (pp. 162-182). Cambridge, MA: Harvard University Press.

White, M. (1995a, September). *Presentation at the Family Institute of Cambridge.* Cambridge, MA.

White, M., & Epston, D. (1990). *Narrative means to therapeutic ends.* New York: Norton.

Wood, A. D. (1973). "The fashionable diseases": Women's complaints and their treatment in nineteenth-century America. *Journal of Interdisciplinary History, 4,* 25-52.

Nobody Tells You Who You Are: First Notes on a Community Project for Girls and Women in Rural Massachusetts

Ellen Pulleyblank

SUMMARY. In spite of many changes for girls and women, research indicates that between the ages of nine and twelve many girls begin to limit their expectations. This is often exacerbated in rural areas where girls have few opportunities. This paper provides the first notes about a rural community project for girls and women. It is a description of a community development process that not only addresses the needs of the girls and the adult women mentors who participate, but also of a network of activities and resources developed by and for the larger community. *[Article copies available for a fee from The Haworth Document Delivery Service: 1-800-342-9678. E-mail address: <getinfo@haworthpressinc.com> Website: <http://www.haworthpressinc.com>]*

KEYWORDS. Women's psychology, community building, rural, girls' development, female adolescence, mentoring programs

INTRODUCTION

As with many other family therapists over the past ten years, my work has been influenced by the ideas of narrative therapy, feminism and the multicul-

---

Ellen Pulleyblank, PhD, is an Adjunct Faculty Member at the Smith College School for Social Work and a Research Fellow at its Center for Innovative Practice.

Address correspondence to: Ellen Pulleyblank, 50 Potash Hill Road, Cummington, MA 01026.

[Haworth co-indexing entry note]: "Nobody Tells You Who You Are: First Notes on a Community Project for Girls and Women in Rural Massachusetts." Pulleyblank, Ellen. Co-published simultaneously in *Journal of Feminist Family Therapy* (The Haworth Press, Inc.) Vol. 11, No. 4, 2000, pp. 47-63; and: *Feminism, Community, and Communication* (ed: Mary E. Olson) The Haworth Press, Inc., 2000, pp. 47-63. Single or multiple copies of this article are available for a fee from The Haworth Document Delivery Service [1-800-342-9678, 9:00 a.m. - 5:00 p.m. (EST). E-mail address: getinfo@haworthpressinc.com].

© 2000 by The Haworth Press, Inc. All rights reserved.

tural critique; all challenging the powerful position of therapist, offering collaboration as an alternative, and demanding that we pay attention to the meanings of social context. I have also been affected by the exhortation of John McKnight (1995) who criticizes those of us in the human professions for defining problems in our clients that in effect disable them and re-route them from their natural community into communities of social services. He believes that we should use our skills to help create opportunities for communities to assess and decide for themselves how to respond to their concerns. Particularly when I work with families facing catastrophic illness, I think of myself more as a convener than as a family therapist (Pulleyblank, 1999). With these ideas in my head, I moved to rural Massachusetts hoping to find ways to live and work in a cultural context that was new to me.

This paper describes how initial chance encounters with my neighbors led to the formation of a community organization we call Sisters Inc. whose first project is designed for girls ages 9-12 and teen and adult mentors. This project is called, "Nobody Tells You Who You Are." It is a work in progress, and this paper attempts to document how it is evolving. At this point in time the project is made up of three separate but linked components that have developed from discussions with women and girls in the Hilltowns of Western Massachusetts. These components are:

- A series of creative arts workshops that use art, improvisational game playing and group discussions as a means of encouraging self-awareness, exploring limiting cultural stereotypes and developing a mentor/mentee relationship.
- Mentor/mentee relationships in which local teens and adult women volunteer to develop one-on-one special relationships with the girls in the program. All girls from 9 to 12 who live in the area are welcome. They come as a result of flyers, school presentations, and referrals from counselors or parent interest. Our only limitation is space and the number of available mentors. The mentors range in age from fourteen to seventy-three. They are local women who hear about the project through word of mouth and volunteer. They say that they are drawn to the project because of their desire to be in relationship to other women and to reach out to young girls in ways that they missed as children. This first year we have thirteen girls and thirteen mentors in the program. The role of the mentors is to encourage the girls to be themselves and to explore opportunities that interest them. The mentors participate in the workshops and invite the girls into their lives. They offer them a wider view of what might be possible for them. Parents participate with the mentors by discussing their concerns and making suggestions about what their daughters need.

- A resource network of other women in the community who have limited time, but who want to be part of the project, participate as members of an advisory board of Sisters Inc. or offer mini-workshops for the girls and the mentors. This year these workshops include: pottery, hide tanning, costume tea parties and bird house building to name but a few of the activities offered.

Since many women in this community are isolated, this program offers an opportunity for us to develop a supportive network for ourselves as well as for the girls. In these early stages of the project all participants are encouraged to make changes as we go along. Mentors are especially encouraged to take responsibility for the development of the program.

BEGINNINGS

For me, this project was a long time in the making and has its roots in my childhood experience as a young girl. When I was nine, I ran and biked through the streets of Jersey City, New Jersey with a pack of boys. I cut my hair short so that they would let me play outfield on the baseball team. I boxed with Marc Goldberg, and he got in trouble when I knocked him down. My mother didn't seem to notice my "ungirlike" behavior until one day when I came home from a baseball game with a chipped tooth. Without any introduction, she began to rant. "You can never play ball with those boys again. You are a girl. What if the ball had hit you in the chest?" In a panic I called my best friend Linda. She and I tried to figure out what was wrong with my mother. A few years later, when we understood better what it meant to be female, we still believed that our mothers had gone mad, never to be cured when issues of femininity or even worse sexuality raised their ugly heads.

Most women have a story about how they entered the world of girls and struggled to find their way into womanhood. Few of the stories that I've heard are joyful. What I learned at that early age was that I could turn to other girls and together we might make some sense of a world that controlled us, but often didn't include us. We all agreed that the world of grownups was to be avoided as we searched for information about how to be female. Most of our mothers in the middle-class Jewish community in which we lived told us that we could be anything that we wanted to be. However, even those who worked full-time, did all the traditional female jobs at home. We, as girls, were expected to follow suit. Our fathers saw us as their little girls, only to be relinquished as little girls upon marriage.

In 1993, my husband of twenty-eight years died. At the age of fifty I found myself on my own for the first time in my life. I had worked outside of our home throughout my marriage and had shared economic and child-care responsibilities with my husband. I thought I was an independent adult. But after my husband died, I discovered that I knew very little about how to live on my own. In 1996, after many confused attempts at establishing a life for myself, I moved across the country to live in Cummington, one of the Hilltowns of Western Massachusetts. Cummington is part of a group of small sparsely settled towns geographically distant from larger population centers. The nearest grocery store of any size is thirty minutes away. These small villages are all about six miles apart and each has a population well under one thousand people. The number of inhabitants hasn't grown since it was settled in the 1700s. Though the population is mostly white, there is a wide mixture of socio-economic and ethnic groups. There are few services or activities. People tend to be friendly when they meet at the Old Creamery, the only store in town, but there is little socializing and significant isolation.

One of the hardest parts of leaving the home that I had known for twenty-five years was the loss of closeness to my women friends. I wondered if I would make new friends at this time of my life. However, by a stroke of good luck, I got to know Deborah Coffey, an artist and teacher who also lives in Cummington. As Deborah and I became friends, we talked about our experiences growing up. On one sunny afternoon as we lay on the grass Deborah suggested that we make collages of what life was like for us as girls. We tore through magazines, pulling out makeup and bra ads and then the counter-images of what we had dreamed to be and to do. We started meeting regularly and made up a game that we called "Nobody Tells You Who You Are." The original idea came from a game called Statues that we had played as children. To play we would join hands and whirl each other around. One of us would take the role of a sculptor, spinning the other one around and then releasing her. Once released, the whirler fell into a pose and froze: Like clay that is thrown. We turned some of the sculptures into characters and created improvised role-play situations for them.

Over the next few months we played the game with each other and with any friends and neighbors who were willing to join in. As the game developed we saw that our practice of characterizing the statues was a way to examine stereotypes that had been imposed on us as girls and that we thought might still be operating on girls' consciousness. We believed that as with the random throwing of the clay, we are all thrown into forms that are perceived and defined by cultural expectations. These expectations often have little to do with who we really are or what we most wish to do with our lives. In order to explore these ideas further, we looked for women and girls from nearby towns who were willing to play the game and also discuss with us their needs and concerns. The game was transformed into the six creative arts workshops that form the basis for our project, "Nobody Tells You Who You Are." Our discussions with them led to the idea of including a mentoring component and a community resource network as interlocking parts of the program. The Women's Fund of Western Massachusetts gave us our initial funding.

THE BIG PICTURE

As we got more interested in the project, our group read some of the current research about girls. We found that though the women's movement has changed many women's lives for the better, adolescent girls are in trouble. Depression, eating disorders, anxiety about physical appearance, and attempted suicide are increasing in this population. An *AAUW* study (1992) of girls aged 9 to 15 found that as girls reach adolescence they experience a significantly greater drop in self-esteem than boys. A poll conducted as part of this study confirmed that girls were systematically, if unintentionally discouraged from a wide range of academic pursuits. These national trends are particularly acute in sparsely settled rural areas due to a lack of organized activities or supports for girls. A local needs assessment of girls aged 6 to 18 conducted by agencies in Western Massachusetts (1999) found that girls need more programs, community groups, places to go, sports and life skills training. Program developers also need to address barriers that keep girls from community participation due to transportation problems, conflict with family responsibilities, cost, and reluctance to try new programs.

Pre-adolescence is a time of particular vulnerability to stress and distress. Research (Brooks-Gunn 1990, Colten & Gore 1991, Werner & Smith 1992) indicates that somewhere between the ages of nine and ten, young girls lose a sense of confidence in themselves. They begin to compare themselves to others and find themselves wanting. They blame themselves for their supposed deficits. They internalize these feelings, rather than protesting against the social pressures that encourage them to conform to a narrow definition of femininity. It is at this age that girls' declining sense of self begins to inhibit their actions and activities. As they withdraw into themselves, girls take less advantage of opportunities even when they are made available. It is also at this age that girls as a group start to do badly in school. Often they have no one to talk to and remain miserable in silence. This negative transformation usually occurs outside of the awareness of the girls, their mothers and other caring adults. It is this research that influenced our decision to work with girls ages nine through twelve.

Our plan for the interlocking parts of the program was influenced by the idea of building a "hardiness zone" for girls. Research (Debold et al. 1998) shows that a girl's well being depends not only on her individual circumstances but also on the nature of her wider social context. Communities that support girls in ways that resist the stress that undermines them and that interferes with their development have been termed by Diebold et al. (1998) as "hardiness zones." These zones provide the conditions for girls to thrive, allowing them to experience a sense of purpose in how they contribute to the community, to become part of a network of relationships, and to recognize that there are resources for their support. Many rural towns, like the ones that this program serves, have few services for girls. When new programs are offered, adults are often slow to take advantage of them, especially in the case of girls. Recently, for example, the Hilltown Family Center began a program for teens. The program is still relatively new, but so far, 26 boys attend regularly while only three girls take part. Breaking this cycle of isolation and self-imposed restrictions is one goal of our project. In this way we have not defined the problem as one that exists in the life of a particular girl, but rather the result of limited information and relationship possibilities affecting all pre-adolescent girls at the local and national level.

The seminal research on hardiness zones initially assessed the absence of resilience in terms of behavioral and relational difficulties more often seen in young boys: disengagement, violence, classroom disruptiveness (Debold 1995: Rutter & Garmezy 1983: Schonert-Reichl & Offer 1992). Girls in early childhood were deemed more resilient *de facto* because they scored low on these indices and also because they were more engaged and sensitive to relationships (Debold 1995). Yet by adolescence, girls' confidence in their relationships suffers as their resilience wanes (Block 1990, Werner & Smith 1982, 1992).

Diebold et al. (1998) state: "Girls' struggles are rooted in systemic problems, such as poverty, racism and sexism, that require collective rather than individual response." They go on to say:

> This suggests a need for a new concept of health and stress resistance that locates the struggles between the girl and her world, not simply within the individual girl, and that holds the adults in girls' environments accountable for providing girls with experiences and opportunities for them to understand and engage with and potentially transform what limits and harms them.

Keeping the notion of a "hardiness zone" in mind, our project, "Nobody Tells You Who You Are" is using a systemic approach to address the needs of girls and women in our community. By combining mentoring relationships, parent and school involvement, and creative arts workshops, we are building a community network that will help girls resist harmful social pressures while providing support for teens and adult women as well. In this way we also hope to support the families of the girls, many of whom encourage their daughters to be themselves, but find that their own busy lives, their cultural context, and the values of the marketplace often subvert their best efforts.

We cannot even assume that the girls in our program have support from other girls in the way that we did at their age. During the workshop discussion groups, the girls in Sisters Inc. talk about their difficulties with other girls. They don't feel there is anyone that they can trust. It seems to them as if one day they have a best friend, and the next day they have no friends at all. They say that they are fearful of telling other girls what they think and feel. According to Resnick et al. (1997), fewer girls in adolescence perceive themselves as connected to their families and school–two of the most important protective factors found in recent research on resilience. One of the initial tentative findings of the workshop evaluations is that in this context, the girls do develop trusting friendships, which, according to reports of their parents, help them stay more involved at home and at school. Clearly these results are anecdotal and only a formal evaluation will tell us how our program is effecting the present lives of girls and whether these effects are sustained throughout high school. We hope to begin a more formal outcome study next year.

THE PROJECT:
NOBODY TELLS YOU WHO YOU ARE

The program begins in the fall. We offer six three-hour creative arts workshops. All the mentors and the girls attend. Parents are invited to the workshops too. Since the workshops are open to anyone who is interested, we often have visitors. The purpose of the creative arts workshops is to give girls at this age tools to resist the social pressures that undermine their self-confidence. In her work as an artist and teacher with girls in grades four through six, my colleague Deborah Coffey found that art is a language that gives them a way of expressing many of the experiences that they may not have words to express. It also offers them a joyful and creative opportunity to share their accomplishments with others, and to be seen and heard more fully than in other parts of their lives.

At the first creative arts workshop, we begin by asking the mentors to remember what it was like for them when they were the same age as the girls. Specifically, we ask them to give examples of when they felt pressured to conform and when they felt free to be most like themselves. One story in particular stands out. Amy, a mentor in her late thirties, tells us that when she was nine a friend of her mother's once or twice took her out, just the two of them. On those outings, Amy says that she felt seen and heard in a different way then in any other part of her life. She still remembers the feelings of pride in being included by an adult woman in this way. After hearing all the mentors' stories we play the Statues game.

The Statues Game

Part 1. In order to teach the game, two mentors are asked to volunteer to play the first round. One woman at a time is gently swung around by a facilitator and let go. She falls into a posture and freezes. The group decides who she is. They call out: "You look like a dancer, a farmer, a rag doll." The group then decides how she should dress. They use materials provided to help her to construct a hat that represents the stereotypical qualities of her character. In this part of the game she has to conform to the group's directions. The group follows this same exercise with the second player and creates a second character.

For example, when playing the game with two girls, the group defines the characters as a rag doll and a cheerleader. Choosing stereotyped characteristics of cheerleaders, the group describes her as amiable, wanting to please, bubbly, happy, always with a smile. The rag doll is described as helpless, indecisive, floppy. The cheerleader is told to put her hair in a ponytail and to decorate her cap with pink pompom balls. The rag doll is told to decorate her hat with floppy pieces of cloth that fall into her face. The cheerleader and the rag doll are then put into a role-playing situation. They are placed on the school bus with only one available seat and have to decide who gets the seat. In this first role-play, the cheerleader acts in her defined role of trying to please and keeps offering the seat to the rag doll. The rag doll can't make up her mind whether or not she wants the seat, but eventually she falls into the seat, almost knocking the cheerleader over. The cheerleader and the rag doll are photographed with a Polaroid camera. They are interviewed about their experience of the role-play. Their comments are written on a large board. They tell us that they had fun, but didn't like being told how to play their parts.

Part 2. In the second phase of the game Deborah and I ask the girls, "If you could change this character, is there something about her that you would change so that she is more like you or more like you would wish her to be in this role?" The cheerleader and the rag doll now get a chance to change their hats to fit their ideas of how they wish the characters to behave and to look. With their new hats they go back into the role-play and play out the scene the way they want it to go, this time without conforming to stereotypes. In this second role-play, they resolve the problem by deciding to sit in the seat together. They act playful with each other. The rag doll keeps falling on the floor and the cheerleader urges her back onto the seat, both of them giggling. Another photograph is taken and they are again asked about their experience of the exercise. This time they say that they had even more fun and like their characters much better.

Group Discussion

Following the game we review the comments that have been recorded during it, and then discuss the following questions with the girls.

1. What does the game have to do with what happens at school?
2. What kind of things do you wish you could do that you stop yourself from doing?
3. How can mothers and mentors help you experiment and be creative in the choices that you make for yourselves?

Outcome

Each girl and her mentor meet to make a pact. They decide how to spend time together in order for the mentor to support the girl in being the kind of person she wishes to be and in doing the things that she wishes to do. The girl-mentor teams announce these plans to the group.

The Creative Arts Workshops

This introductory game leads to the development of characters that form the basis for the creative arts workshops. Some girls choose their own characters. Others develop the characters that the group identified for them in the Statues game. They make hats for them and two masks; one face for what the girls believe their characters show in compliance with what is expected of them and another face that their characters wish to hide. Finally each girl makes a standing life-size figure of her character in plywood. These figures are painted by the girls in ways that show both the stereotypical aspects of the character and the parts that are kept hidden. The cheerleader, for example, has a red and blue bouncy costume, covered with pom-pom. A prison is painted on her chest. Trapped inside the prison is the face of a small-frightened girl. The girls excitedly introduce these figures at the final workshop. The character's names are called out: "Artemis," "Sunray," "Billy," "Cockichoa," "Buzz," etc., each girl embodying her character with name, sound and gesture.

At this final workshop Deborah and I wonder what the workshops, mentoring relationships and mini-workshops mean to the girls and to the mentors. We know that attendance at the workshops was high throughout the year. No one dropped out. In the evaluations of each workshop, the girls and mentors stated that they liked what we were doing, but we want to know more about how they think about what we have done together. We ask the girls and mentors to tell us about their experiences in Sisters Inc. Following the excitement and noise about the figures, this question quiets the circle, but slowly the girls and mentors speak up.

The Girls

> I liked sliding around on your floor while we baked bread. I'm not used to being with grownups who don't make a lot of rules.
>
> I liked pulling hides, which was very yucky, but something I've never done before.
>
> I liked being with my mentor who would just listen to me and do special things with me.
>
> In the workshops I could speak out in this large group when I've never felt comfortable in any group.
>
> I felt included when I've mostly felt left out.
>
> Here, I want to show people what I do when usually I act like I don't care what other people think about me.
>
> I was not so worried about my friends at school because I knew that I had friends here.

The Mentors

> I loved walking in the woods when my mentee was leading the way.
>
> I enjoyed the trips we took to museums. I did things I wouldn't ordinarily take the time to do.
>
> I marveled at the girls' creativity and they encouraged me to be creative myself.
>
> I've met women I never would have met before.
>
> Sometimes I got to feel like nine years old again.

As Deborah and I look around the circle, we notice the difference between this workshop and our first meeting. At our first workshop when the girls were asked to introduce themselves with a sound and a gesture, the first girl said her name, waved and said, "Hi." Everyone copied her. No one dared to stand out. The mentors and the girls were awkward with each other, kept separate by age and assumed roles. Now everyone is at ease, mixing with each other, speaking out openly in the group.

As a finale for the year we all prepare for a community exhibition of our artwork. We display the hats, masks and figures that we made. In addition, the girls, with the help of their mentors, create display tables that show the things in their lives that matter to them the most. At the exhibition most of the girls give performances. The girls without adults design these performances. We in the audience are surprised by their sense of fun despite their lack of polish and their freedom to show us what they enjoy.

In order to continue learning about the experience of the girls and mentors in Sisters Inc., we interview some of them after the exhibition is over. Here is an example of one set of those interviews.

MENTOR/MENTEE VIEW: TWO INTERVIEWS

Gloria-A Mentor

Gloria sits comfortably in my living room sipping cold water. Her long dark hair, only slightly flecked with gray, is pulled back from her strong face. She wears comfortable clothes, looking country-casual like most of the women in Cummington. Her brightly patterned shirt reflects her vibrancy at age 73. She has lived for many years in this community and knows its history well. She has done various jobs in her life, and now retired, she continues to write. She responds to my questions about her impressions of Sisters Inc.:

> When I think about my year with Sisters Inc. I see a confusing maze of different impressions. Intellectually, I approve of what we are trying to do, but I often felt unsure of what I should be doing or if I was doing it right. I remember being nine. Adults were in another world. When I think about my mother, I know we were close, but it was my job to take care of her. It's funny how memories come back. I remember when I was about nine and I had a part in a play all the way across town. It was 1936. We lived in Baltimore in a row house with mostly African-American families as neighbors. My father was the manager of the local Kenny shoe store. In those days only a white man could be a manager, but we were still very poor. My mom was agoraphobic, only no one called it that then. She just always stayed at home. So when it was time for me to play an elf across town, I put on my purple elf suit and took

the trolley on my own. When I think back, I am very proud of that little girl who was so scared that she might miss her stop that she got off blocks ahead of time and walked the rest of the way alone through an unfamiliar neighborhood. I also feel angry with my mother. Things weren't always right back then. A lot was expected of us while our parents struggled in worlds that we knew nothing about.

I write furiously trying to keep up with Gloria's story. So much of what we hope to do with the project is to learn about each other as women and then to become part of the lives of some of the young girls in our community. I realize that this first year we haven't spent nearly enough time getting to know each other. When I mention this to Gloria she agrees with me.

> In these Hilltowns there is a lot of isolation. It wasn't always that way, but many new people have moved in. I used to show up at new peoples' doors with my sour cream coffeecake, but often people seemed uncomfortable, waiting for me to leave. I don't do that any more. I'm hoping to break through some of that isolation by building relationships with other mentors.

I ask her what it was like to be a mentor:

> It helped me a lot when I learned to let the silence between Amber (her mentee) and me just happen. It also worked to invite her into my life. One of our best times together was when she came with my husband and me to pick up our new dog Mordecai. We all went to the pound. We were very excited and she helped us figure out what Mordecai needed in his new home. She and I also had a great time going to a mini-workshop where we learned to make pottery together. The hardest part was doing art with her at the workshops. She is so much freer and better than I am in that area. I often found myself just standing by and watching her with awe.

Gloria and I then eat sweet Queen Ann cherries and gossip about our lives. We give each other a big hug as she gets ready to leave. It is a series of meetings like this that has sustained me during the transition into my new home.

Amber–A Mentee

A few days later on a late summer afternoon, Amber's mother drives her over to my house. She drops her off saying that she'll be back in about an hour. After she leaves, Amber and I awkwardly try to decide where we should go for our talk. I feel the silence that Gloria had described earlier. I suggest to Amber that we sit on a large rock in front of my house that overlooks the meadow. We walk over to the rock, sit down and look out onto the meadow without saying much. I break our silence by telling Amber about this article that I am writing. She brightens up and looks more interested in our conversation.

Amber is a tall sturdy young girl with summer-cropped hair, blue jean overalls and for today's visit blue eye shadow, blue nail polish and blue lipstick. I remember that when she had her hair cut for the summer, one of the girls said that she looked like a boy. Without much distress she said that it worked well for swimming and would be all grown back in the fall. During the workshops Amber was often quiet, but always focused and involved in her projects. At the final exhibition, she gave a lecture about the best ways to make clay figures. She explained in great detail what she had learned about clay at the mini-workshop that she and Gloria attended with a local potter as an adjunct activity to Sisters Inc. Her favorite interest was bugs, and the character that she created was an entomologist named Buzz, who showed everyone her excitement about bugs, but hid her fear of being bitten by an unknown species.

I ask Amber what she likes best about Sisters Inc. She says:

> I like meeting new girls and making new friends who aren't from my school. I also got to do creative things that I don't usually do. In school we don't get much time to work on art projects. It's also fun going to other people's houses. Even when we baked cookies that didn't come out we had fun. I also got to make clay figures for my ladybug cage and for my sister.

As quickly as she begins, Amber stops talking and there we are again in silence. This time I feel more comfortable just sitting there with her for awhile and then without much effort we get to talking about the things that she usually does at home.

> My Grandma lives up the road and so does my best friend Amanda. There is a river next to Amanda's house and we go after river clams with sticks. I ride my bike to her house and to my grandparent's house almost every day. My Grandma and Grandpa have a big L on their chimney for our last name. I ride up to bring them the newspaper in the mornings. I also play a lot with my sister.

She takes a breath, and I ask her about her parents.

> The grown-ups at my house are pretty busy and I do a lot of jobs. I'm the oldest so I have a lot of responsibilities. Sometimes that makes me

grumpy, but most of the time I don't mind. I sometimes make money babysitting or selling black raspberries. I only spend the money on what I need and try to help my family buy things.

Our conversation rambles on and then Amber tells me about the boys:

I can ask my Mom any questions I have about boys, but I didn't talk much about them with Gloria. Most of the boys at school are riff-raff. Only the bad girls go with the boys otherwise the boys and girls keep separate, unless you're a couple. There is a boy I like and he's different. We're good friends, but we only see each other at school.

Finally we talk about Sisters Inc. next year.

I want to keep Gloria as my mentor. I really like our one-on-one time together. We do special things. I like that she spends time with me and isn't too busy. I hope we get to do some of the same things next year. Maybe my friend Amanda will join.

Our conversation runs out of steam so I suggest that we go into the house and have milk and cookies. Shortly thereafter Amber's mother joins us. The silence has disappeared and we easily chat about summer and then about the coming of fall. In these rural towns the seasons mark the quality of our lives. Amber's mother lets me know that she is very happy with the program for Amber and that she appreciates having Gloria in their lives. She tells me that some of the load of her busy life is lifted with the help of another caring adult in the life of her daughter.

As with the evaluations of the workshops these interviews seem to indicate that we are building a hardiness zone for girls in our community. The girls feel freer to express themselves. They are contributing to their community and see themselves as connected to a supportive network of relationships. Their parents and mentors are part of this network and benefit from it as well. Their teachers and school counselors tell us that they notice the difference in the girls who participate. They plan to tell more girls about the program next year. This like other indications of what may be the results of the program will take further study.

FUTURE PLANS

We recently had a meeting of last year's mentors to do some planning. One of our main concerns is building a network of mentors that view mentoring as part of their lives in an ongoing way rather than in connection to any one girl. It will take a core of people to sustain the program. Many programs fail because they are attached to leaders rather than to the community. We hope to avoid this outcome by developing the program with the participants as we go along. Deborah and I hope to give it away to the community within three or four years. We will then participate like other mentors rather than as leaders.

At the mentors' meeting, they tell us that though they enjoyed last year's program they need more opportunities to bring their creativity into the workshops. Some suggestions from the mentors are very specific. Mary says:

> I'd like us to have a more organized beginning and ending to the workshops, perhaps some simple ritual would call us together and then at the end mark what we have done. We could even do a ritual around clean-up.

Stephanie says:

> I want it to be ok during the workshops to hang out with other mentors. I always felt as if I wasn't supposed to be talking with them, but that's one of the things that I enjoyed the most. I'd also like us to sing more and to read stories together.

Other ideas float in and out of our conversation:

> Let's use community resources to consult with us about mentor-mentee projects.

> Let's develop different circles for reading, outdoor adventures, movement whatever.

> Let's encourage each mentor to bring into the workshop her particular form of creativity. Even if someone doesn't want to do the art activity they could use another form to chronicle the workshop from a different point of view with film or a narrative or whatever interests them.

> Let's make time just for the mentors at the beginning of each workshop. This would give the girls a picture of our commitment to ourselves and will show them our solidarity.

The mentors agree to make calls to recruit new mentors for this year. They will invite them to the mentor training. Deborah and I decide that we will also be mentors next year so that we will be more part of the group and begin to move away from our leadership positions.

What we are learning most about is how to build a program in our community that isn't for a special group of girls with "special needs." None of the girls has a problem. However, they all live in a social context in which they are inhibited by social pressures that they do not know how to resist and that interfere with their development. Creating what we mean by a hardiness zone here in the Hilltowns, one that changes this context with the women and girls who live here, is still new for us. For next year as a result of the mentoring meetings we've had so far, we've made the following plans:

- to use the first forty-five minutes of each workshop for the mentors only, as a way of building our group cohesion.
- to emphasize in the workshops the idea of fluid teams coming together for different purposes and contrast this with the formation of cliques that exclude people.
- to add a community service component with the help of two students from Smith College who will work with the teen mentors to develop this part of the program.
- to focus on the world of work of the women who present the mini-workshops.
- to share the responsibility of writing a narrative of our process as we go along.
- to continue developing a funding base that supports what we want to do.

Since this project is a work in progress, its form will continue to change with the people who participate and the knowledge that we gain as we move along. Just yesterday as I was finishing this piece we were told that we will get funding from the local Community Development Corporation. The project will also change as we move from a mainly volunteer organization to a partially funded one. How we maintain our connection to what we in the community want, rather than be pulled by what funders want, is still to be seen. Without careful study it is hard to know if what we are doing makes a difference. For now we are satisfied with the excitement that we feel and the growing support from a wider and wider circle of people in our community. I believe that I am learning how to use my skills not from the vantage point of a professional outsider, but as a member of the group with whom I can share my expertise, as well as my concerns.

REFERENCES

AAUW Report (1992). *How Schools Shortchange Girls*. Washington, D.C: American Association of University Women Foundation,

Block, J. (1990, October). Ego resilience through time: Antecedents and ramifications. In *Resilience and psychological health. Symposium of the Boston Psychoanalytic Society,* Boston, MA.

Brooks-Gunn, J. & Reiter, E.O. (1990). The role of pubertal processes. In S.S. Feldman & G. Elliott (Eds.), *At the Threshold* (pp.16-53). Cambridge, MA: Harvard University Press

Brown, L.M. (1998) *The politics of girls' anger: Class accents and white femininities.* Cambridge, MA: Harvard University Press.

Brown, L.M. & Gilligan, C. (1992) *Meeting at the crossroads.* Cambridge, MA: Harvard University Press.

Colten, M. E. & Gore, S. (Eds.). (1991) *Adolescent stress.* New York: Aldine de Gruyter.

Debold, E. (1995). *Body politic: Transforming adolescent girl's health.* A report of the 1994 proceedings of the Healthy Girls/Healthy Women Research Roundtable: New York: Ms. Foundation for Women

Debold, E., L.M. Brown, S. Weseen & G.K., Brookins. (1998) Cultivating Hardiness Zones for Adolescent Girls: A Reconceptualization of Resilience in Relationships with Caring Adults. In *Beyond Appearance: A new look at adolescent girls* (in press) Washington, D.C.: APA Publications.

Girls Inc., Western Massachusetts, Pioneer Valley Girl Scout Council, YWCA of Western Massachusetts, The Care Center. *(1999.)* Girls' Needs in Franklin, Hampden, and Hampshire Counties. Northampton: MA. Market Street Research, Inc.

McKnight, J. (1995) *The Careless Society.* New York: Basic Books.

Orenstein, P. (1994) *Schoolgirls.* New York: Doubleday.

Pulleyblank, E (1999) Sending out the call: Community as a source of healing. *Families, Systems and Health: Journal of Collaborative Health Care.* Winter, Vol.17, Number 4.

Rutter, M. & Garmezy, N. (1983) Developmental psychopathology. In P. Mussen, (Ed.), Handbook of child psychology, E.M. Hetherington (vol.ed.) *Socialization, personality and social development* 4 (pp.775-911). New York: Wiley.

Schonert-Reichl, K.A. & Mullen, J. (1996). Correlates of help-seeking in adolescence. *Journal of Youth and Adolescence.* 25, 705-731.

Werner, E. & Smith, R.S. (1982). *Vulnerable but invincible: A longitudinal study of resilient children and youth.* New York: McGraw-Hill.

Werner, E. & Smith, R.S. (1992). *Overcoming the odds: High risk children from birth to adulthood.* Ithaca, NY: Cornell University Press.

Can You Love Them Enough? Organizational Consulting as a Spiritual Quest

Patricia Romney

SUMMARY. This paper describes the labor of the heart for those consulting on contested terrain. A loving practice, it is suggested, can sustain the consultant and potentially heal the organization. *[Article copies available for a fee from The Haworth Document Delivery Service: 1-800-342-9678. E-mail address: <getinfo@haworthpressinc.com> Website: <http://www.haworthpressinc.com>]*

KEYWORDS. Black love, organizational consulting, spirituality

> Hope is an orientation of the Spirit.
>
> –Vaclav Havel

SPIRITUALITY AND LOVE IN ORGANIZATIONS

As anyone who has practiced the art of loving knows, love is something one strives to achieve and maintain not something one falls into.[1] A spiritual

---

Patricia Romney, PhD, is a Clinical and Organizational Psychologist and is President of Romney Associates, Inc., a research and consulting firm.

Address correspondence to: Patricia Romney, 64 Carriage Lane, Amherst, MA 01002 (E-mail: promney@romneyassoc.com).

The author wishes to thank Lynn Hoffman for her "generous reading" of earlier drafts of this paper.

[Haworth co-indexing entry note]: "Can You Love Them Enough? Organizational Consulting as a Spiritual Quest." Romney, Patricia. Co-published simultaneously in *Journal of Feminist Family Therapy* (The Haworth Press, Inc.) Vol. 11, No. 4, 2000, pp. 65-81; and: *Feminism, Community, and Communication* (ed: Mary E. Olson) The Haworth Press, Inc., 2000, pp. 65-81. Single or multiple copies of this article are available for a fee from The Haworth Document Delivery Service [1-800-342-9678, 9:00 a.m. - 5:00 p.m. (EST). E-mail address: getinfo@haworthpressinc.com].

© 2000 by The Haworth Press, Inc. All rights reserved.

orientation to the concept of love requires an appreciation of love as verb-and-object, a joining that ultimately transforms the subject. Love transforms the seeker so that what is achieved is not only the possession of the loved object, but also the fullest possible expression of one's self[2] as a loving being.

In the medieval story of the Quest for the Holy Grail, the Grail or Chalice is what is sought and what is to be achieved is the regeneration of life. The force out of which life regenerates is known to us all as love. Love is the quest that transforms the pilgrim into the object for which he has searched. The quest, then, is a pilgrimage made in order to find the fullest bloom of the Self.

In his comprehensive review of the religious and psychological roots of the meaning of love, Paul Fleischman (1989), a clinical psychiatrist, tells us that "in Buddhism, love is understood as embracing all beings . . . " (p. 190). Jesus, Dr. Fleischman reminds us "preached an unqualified human love: Love your enemies, bless them that curse you . . . if ye salute your brethren only, what do ye more than others?" (p. 190).

Fleischman also reminds us that for Erich Fromm, giving is the essence of love: "a correct giving that doesn't create indebtedness, but creates others who feel they now also have enough extra to give"(p. 197). As Fromm put it, "Love is a power which produces love" (p. 199). As noted above, the subject and the object are the same.

From Paul Fleischman's point of view, "Every case of psychotherapy, to a greater or lesser extent, is a problem of the failure to love" (p. 187). Might the same be said of organizations that seek consultation? Organizational behavior consultants receive calls for assistance with handling conflict, managing diversity, improving staff morale, increasing commitment to the organization's mission and vision, and building cooperative, productive teams. In the domain of organizational behavior, as in the world of psychotherapy, the failure to love is often at the root of these needs and problems.

Contemporary organizational theorists and writers embrace spirituality as an important aspect of organizational life. Manz, Manz, Marx and Neck (in press) examine the spiritual virtues of five Old Testament leaders and use these principles to help business leaders reconcile "business values with virtuous living." Robert Quinn (1996) in his book about organizational change tells us that "Ultimately, deep change, whether at the personal or the organizational level, is a spiritual process" (p. 78). Laurie Beth Jones' *Jesus CEO: Using Ancient Wisdom for Visionary Leadership* (1995) speaks of love as guiding Christ's plans. Writing of the importance of relationships in Jesus' plan, she describes his love for his disciples, and his ability to love them until the end as crucial to his work. "Love," says Jones, " is the infrastructure of everything and anything worthwhile" (p. 255). As Christopher O'Rourke (1997) suggests in his work on group psychotherapy, "listening for the sacred" is an invitation to "encounter the divine." This invitation is important in organizational consulting as well.

Leroy Wells, Jr. (1978) writes that all collaboration between organizations and consultants demands knowledge of organizational systems and the levels of group processes. He identifies five levels of organizational process: intrapersonal, interpersonal, group (group-as-a-whole), intergroup, interorganizational. At all of these levels, cohesion and wholeness are possible, as are conflict and disharmony (splitting). When there is conflict at the intergroup level, the members of the organization may be said to be functioning on what I call *contested terrain*.[3]

CONTESTED TERRAIN IN ONE ORGANIZATION: A PARABLE

In the fall of 1996, an organization that cared for elderly disabled people requested consultation from an Organizational Consultant who was an African American woman. The staff of the organization numbered 1,250. The Director was a man of Moroccan descent. All of the senior mangers were white. Almost all the service delivery staff were "non-Caucasian," and at least half spoke English as a second language. The vast majority of staff were people of African descent, mainly Haitian immigrants. The agency served a population of 450 patients who lived at the facility and were all white.

The Director summarized the issues of contested terrain by saying that the various cultures in his organization had difficulty relating to each other. He described the patients as a "sensory deficit population" and said that caretakers compounded the problem by speaking French and Creole to them instead of English. This worried him, and some of the patients' families had complained. There were also many communication obstacles among factions on the staff. Sometimes there were open affronts, sometimes the barriers were acted out in body language.

The Director explained further that the organization was in the process of downsizing since many clients were being placed out in the community. Staff were "being involuntarily laid off," and were feeling that the administration was "insensitive." "Staff," he said, "want to be treated with respect," and he wanted that too, but as a result of a directive from those above him, he was letting people go.

There were many distressing incidents. In one case an African American staff member said that a manager had pushed and shoved him and had spoken to him in a disparaging way. Another Black staff member complained that a white nurse referred to her as "this girl." In one sector of the organization, the service staff complained of mistreatment by their manager and submitted a petition with 120 signatures.

The Director initially asked the Consultant for help in developing a more open communication style and to build team spirit among staff. Early on, the Consultant attended a meeting of the senior management team. With the exception of the Director, all members of the team were white. After the Consultant was introduced, and issues of conflict between cultural groups and people at different levels in the agency were described several managers expressed an interest in having the Consultant work with them. One wanted help with his staff and another requested focus groups for her program.

Toward the end of the meeting, one manager, who had been silent, declared "Affirmative action hasn't worked." She said she was "tired of quotas," and "positions being held." When the Consultant inquired about quotas and the holding of positions at the agency, she replied that these policies did not apply to their organization, but that she had seen examples in many other places.

In a private meeting with the Consultant, one manager shared the details of an "impasse." A white nurse had complained of a threat from a Haitian staff member and the incident was under investigation. The threat was reportedly verbal, taking the form of the statement: "You don't know who you're dealing with." This statement was interpreted by the nurse as implying that there would be a reprisal. The union had become involved and the nurse had acquired an attorney. Other staff were drawn in, too. During the investigation, one person said that the nurse perceived herself as superior to others and the Director was seen as siding with the staff. In these and similar ways, the investigation had exacerbated tension in all sectors of the agency.

The agency requested a proposal for consultation to deal with these issues, and the Consultant prepared one and handed it in. No response was received for several months. Upon inquiring about the reason for the delay, the Consultant was informed that the Director had left the organization. It was later revealed that he had been terminated.

Nine months later, the new Director, a white woman, contacted the Consultant again. This time she requested another proposal to deal with the same issues. It was written and sent. There was no further word until two months had passed. At that time, an emissary from the organization was sent to meet with the Consultant. In this meeting the Consultant was informed that one problem he saw was that all-Black service delivery staff were being ghettoized into the bottom service delivery level. In addition, disciplinary actions had increased markedly over a three-year period. A class-action suit on behalf of the staff had been filed, claiming mistreatment by managers. Downsizing continued.

A month later the proposal was accepted in writing. The consultation was scheduled to begin in six weeks, despite what the Director described as her managers' "mixed reviews" about whether to go ahead. Three months later, after complicated negotiations and a reduced dollar amount due to the late start, the consultation began. The Consultant's primary objective was to assess the needs of the Center and then to establish support for a Diversity Initiative. The work began with the Consultant using the familiar technology of organizational diagnosticians–observations, individual interviews, focus groups. By the winter of 1998, the organizational assessment was at its midpoint. At this point, one member of the organization termed the organization a "powder keg." Some people were open to the consultation, but others were extremely ambivalent about it, and their silence covered feelings of panic and fear.

The Consultant found it increasingly difficult to operate in this atmosphere. On one occasion during a focus group comprised of managers of the physical plant and technical services, race and racism were discussed. Approximately thirteen managers were present. The staff were all white and predominantly male, except for one manager who was Asian. The Consultant and a Black man who was Co-Chair of the Diversity Committee that was spearheading the Initiative were facilitating the meeting.

The managers described the non-white service delivery staff as not caring about the patients, stealing from them and neglecting them. On the other hand, they maintained that they were color-blind. The conversation grew heated. A few of the white managers asserted that racism was a thing of the past. When the Consultant and the Co-Chair brought up examples of racism, like slavery or the dragging murder of James Byrd in Texas, the managers dismissed these examples as either too old or extreme. When the Co-Chair tried to give an example in the agency, a white manager arose from his chair, leaned across the conference table, pointed his finger in the face of the Black man, and said, "You're a racist." At the request of the Consultant, he later apologized.

In another meeting, a white clinician expressed his resentment about having to "water down" his reports so that they could be understood by staff members whose first language was not English. He asked, "Why do I have to water down my reports so they can be understood by people with a third grade education?" He repeated this comment three times angrily. Haitian staff later met with the Consultant and demanded an apology, which was never received. Threats were reportedly made against the clinician.

The Consultant also met with the service staff. In one of these meetings, a Haitian woman took the floor. Apologizing for her accent, she said she wanted "to say something," in the hope that we "could understand" her. She spoke about how she and her fellow co-workers often felt about their jobs as caretakers. In halting, heavily accented English, she told how they hated to come to work in the morning and how they were unable to speak up for themselves, for fear of retaliation by their supervisors. "Even in meetings when we are asked to talk, we cannot speak," she said. "We are afraid. We get sick. This not speaking makes us sick, because we must hold it inside. We cannot let it out."

She spoke of how she and other direct care workers were ignored: "You are treated like a chair or a table, a piece of furniture. They don't speak to you. You are looked down on, talked down to." She continued, "Those of us who have so small jobs are not respected by those who do big jobs." She said repeatedly, "Even the Bible says we should respect one another. Even the Bible says this."

The Consultant was not exempt from this atmosphere. The concept of parallel process informs us that when the organization is caught up in strife, conflict within the organization will be reflected in conflict between the Consultant and individual members, groups or even the organization as a whole. In fact, the Consultant was screamed at in one meeting, and asked, "Who do you think you are?" On another occasion, her facilitation of a meeting was interrupted, and she was blamed for the intergroup conflict. Finally all the Consultant's records were subpoenaed by the courts as evidence in the suit against the organization. The court was now another entity in the contested terrain.

The Consultant's optimism and confidence were shaken. Could organizational consulting, which attempts to address problems and resolve conflicts in a rational, collaborative way, really be helpful in untangling the hurts and horrors of injustice at the level of whole classes, whole ethnic groups, whole peoples?

FINDING A LOVING STANCE

To go on in my own voice,[4] the organization described above was not easy for me to love. On many occasions, I was moved to anger, on many others I was moved to tears. Like the pilgrim in Rilke's poem *"Ich bete wieder, du Erlaughter,"* overwhelmed by the perilous quest for organizational change in the contested terrain of this organization, I felt moved to cry out:

> I've been scattered in pieces,
> torn by conflict,
> mocked by laughter,
> washed down by drink.
>
> In alleyways I sweep myself up
> Out of garbage and broken glass.

On the occasion when staff members were harangued with reminders of their supposed "third grade education," I drove home weeping. As I wept I remembered a question that Leroy Wells had put to me almost twenty years earlier: "Can you love them enough to help them learn?" I was expressing my frustration about an organization I was consulting to at the time. I have long since forgotten the particular dynamics of the situation, but the question returned to me with full force in the cold winter of 1998.

To understand the question it would help to describe my relationship with Leroy Wells. During his life Wells had been a faculty member at Howard University, a highly influential organizational consultant and creator of the "Black Love" Workshops. His book chapter "The Group-as-Whole: A Systemic Socio-Analytic Perspective on Interpersonal and Group Relations" (1980) was frequently reprinted. According to Clay Alderfer (1999) who remembers Wells as a man of "profound human compassion," this article "remains today one of the most frequently cited theoretical papers in applied behavioral science."

I attended a "Black Love Workshop" facilitated by Wells at The Association of Black Psychologists (ABPsi) annual meeting in Boston in 1975. I met him several years later during the late 1970s when I was a psychology intern at Yale University Medical School. By 1979, Leroy Wells, who was eight years younger than I, had become a friend, and a mentor. When I became Director of the Afro-American Cultural Center at Yale, the home of the Black Church at Yale, Leroy and I were both members of the Church. We co-facilitated a Black Church at Yale retreat and did a couple of other workshops together. Wells was then a doctoral student at Yale's School of Organization and Management, and was already a gifted consultant and teacher. Like the best kind of mentors, his question, "Can you love them enough to help them learn?" encouraged me toward higher ground. Higher ground as he demonstrated in his workshops was a hallowed place where heart, spirit, and mind could meet as one.

In a paper published after his death, Wells (1999) described the work of the consultant or "group-taker." He wrote,

> The consultant must understand the heart of the group (i.e., the core of the group's experience), take the group to heart (i.e., give undivided attention to the group), possess heart (i.e., have the courage to steadfastly work to understand the group), and carry the group in his or her heart (i.e., constantly keep the group as a beloved object).

"The work of the heart," he said,

> is to develop the passion, courage, and compassion to engage in a deeply contactful relationship with the group. (p. 383)

Comparing the role of consultants to that of nautical navigators, Wells said, "Heart is analogous to loran (*long range navigation*) that establishes the geographical location and the direction of the vessel. The group-taker must use empathy to help locate the group in its current voyage" (p. 383). Observing that working with groups is based on the ancient Greek concept of agape, he wrote, "Love for mankind (sic) is the source of the group-taker's courage. Love of learning is the source of the group-taker's commitment. Love and wonder of being fully human is the source of the group-taker's competence" (p. 389). To me, these words of Leroy Wells describe fully the relationship between consulting and loving.

The consultation described above was a difficult one for me. I was ambivalent about accepting the contract, and for eighteen months I was haunted by the idea that the most ethical thing for me to do was to resign. In a time of deep conflict, Wells' question, "Can you love them enough to help them learn?" gave me a way to proceed with integrity and love. Here are some of the ideas I developed as a result of considering his question.

The Idea of a Quest

First, I needed to understand that the question. "Can you love them enough to help them learn?" serves to notify the Consultant of the beginning of a quest. To Quest, the transitive verb, is defined by the Oxford Dictionary as "to search for, pursue, seek out." The suffix "-ion" forms a substantive of condition or action. As a separate word, however, "ion" means "an electrically charged atom or group of atoms." In this sense, then, the Consultant's quest resembles a heat-seeking force, seeking out the love in service of the work.

In a quest the learning process is integral to the outcome. As I, and several of my colleagues, illustrated in an earlier paper (Romney et al., 1992), "Process can be destructive when we lose sight of the . . . potential for learning, growth and change" (p. 98). A positive process means "being committed to (learners') growth and development." In a quest for learning, relationship is also key. Writing in that paper about teaching in the classroom, we asserted "the relationship of the content to oneself, the student-teacher relationship, and the relationships between students are key in the educational endeavor"(p. 98). Considering process and relationship in the case described above, the Consultant was moved from wondering "How can I change them?" to "How can I love them?"

The Importance of Questions

Questions, as Socrates demonstrated centuries ago, have an incredible ability to educate (to lead out) and, in the case of organizations so torn apart, to lead the consultant up to higher ground. The question "Can you love them enough to help them learn?" demands a response of continuing to question. Am I loving them enough? Am I helping them to learn? Will I? What does it mean for me to love them? How much is enough? What do I have to do to help them learn? Who are they? If I am to help, how? What is my role? Am I able? What must I do to be able?

Such questions push learners to ask what makes a question transformative. In analyzing Wells' question to me, I saw that the question was phrased in such a way as to encourage agency and to inspire a reach. The phrase, "Can you . . ." located the responsibility for the outcome in my sphere of influence.

Second, the question "*Can* you" was oriented toward possibility thinking. Is it possible for you to be able to consider doing this? Even if I were not capable of it at the time, the question asked me to entertain the idea that I could do so. I was reminded of Norman Vincent Peale's famous quote, "Raise your sights and see possibilities–always see them, for they're always there."

Third, the question was phrased so that it generated the "not yet said." Considering the "not yet said" in this organization helped me to look with a compassionate eye toward the organization and to ask, "What is the pain that leads people to behave in this way?"

The Importance of Wonder

Another word related to questioning is wonder. Wonder, with its two handmaidens, awe and reverence, unites inquiry and love. When these two ideas are brought together in work with an organization, another manifestation of love is possible.

When I thought about the pain of people in the organization and attempted to maintain a reverence for their humanity, I understood how downsizing had struck fear into everyone's hearts. Service delivery staff, being at the bottom, were naturally worried, but so were the white managers. Many of them were people in their fifties who had worked at the Center since they were young college students. Where would they go next? They saw the world around them changing, and they did not understand why or how. They felt themselves becoming anachronistic, as white workers in a residential facility at a time when community integration was becoming the norm and organizations were increasingly being called to hire people of color. The litigation taking place frightened them further. They felt wrongly accused and many spent sleepless nights worrying about the outcome of these complaints. They were worried and they were angry. The combination of fear and anger created a defensiveness and an aggressiveness of which they themselves were not often aware.

In contested terrain, the consultant's work is to encourage enough empathy to allow the competing groups to release their hold on the negative and replace it with something positive. Loving people means taking them up to higher ground when, for fear of losing all, they hold on with iron-fisted desperation to the little that they have. A loving practice means that the vision must be conceived under spiritual guidance.

Wonder is one of those spiritual gifts that the consultant can impart. It is like the wonder that is created by seeing or feeling the art of Karen Spitzberg, the "visual artist" who creates art for blind people. Spitzberg, who teaches art history and art appreciation to people who are blind, creates work to be touched. Art, she tells us, is in the fingertips and in the mind. In a similar vein, the consultant can bring to organizations an awareness that they have not had before; she can teach them to "see" even when they have for so long been blind.

Looking for the Exceptions

Love, in contested terrain, also means looking for the "exceptions" (Steve de Shazer, 1994) and "unique outcomes" (Michael White, 1995). It means finding the times when the dehumanization is not present, when the strength and the competencies of the "other" are seen. In this case, the Consultant looked for staff members who were exceptions to the examples described above. One question to ask is, "Who is enacting the holy?"[5] This meant directing my attention to staff who were able to engage in some kind of respectful, loving practice with others. I found this ability in many of the members of the Diversity Committee, and in the Assistant Director of the facility and in the Director.

In the beginning of the second year of the consultation, I met with the Director, the Assistant Director and the Equal Opportunity Officer from the Central Office. I was not pleased with the meeting. Throughout the consultation all contacts with the agency had been initiated by the Consultant or by the Central Office Equal Opportunity Officer, who had strongly recommended that the organization seek consultation. Because the agency, itself, never initiated contact, I believed they did not see themselves as partners in the enterprise. It was as if it were the Consultant's project, not theirs.

Second, the organization wanted to remove the Assistant Director from her position as co-chair of the Diversity Committee, on the grounds that she was too busy. I knew this would give the committee the message that the Initiative was no longer considered important. Third, I believed the organization continued to avoid looking at changes in policy and climate, preferring to focus on seemingly easier solutions of training and diversity celebrations.

I decided to ask the Director to meet me for lunch outside the facility. I hoped that if we were able to talk person to person, we would be able to develop more trust and better collaboration. I began the meeting by saying to the Director, "I'm confused. Who am I working for? You or the people from Central Office?" After her initial surprise, and the revelation that she thought it was I who continued to involve Central Office, the Director assured me that I was working for her and for her agency. This exchange removed us from a triangulation that had interfered with the work. Seeing me as paired with Central Office made it difficult for us to develop a partnership. Without the presence of the higher authorities in our meeting, she and I began to develop a more productive relationship.

Our next topic was the Assistant Director who wanted to step down from her position as co-chair of the Diversity Committee. She was being mentored by the Director, and I shared my enthusiasm about her. I explained how much she was respected by all staff and how much integrity she had. Like the Director, I saw her tremendous leadership potential and I told the Director that I had some specific plans for developing it. I also told her that I saw Diversity work as crucial to all managers' learning. My goals and the Director's goals converged again, strengthening our ability to collaborate.

We next talked about how to give the Diversity Committee a specific task that would allow them to see their importance in the work and have an experience of accomplishment. The Director also invited the Consultant to help her think about how to design a mentoring program for new managers at the facility, and ended the meeting by opening her arms to the Consultant to offer her a hug. The agency had finally welcomed the Consultant and was beginning to join in the work.

I found other examples of "exceptions" in the patients themselves. Although the previous Director and other managers and patients had complained about Haitian staff speaking Creole in front of the patients, we noted that there were some "unique outcomes" (White, 1995). In some cases staff would sing lullabies and other songs from their childhood to their patients. These tunes offered comfort and joy. Observers would notice that even non-verbal patients, or those who spoke only English, would often respond to their caretakers if they were spoken to in Creole. A chair would be moved, a plate carried to the table, or there would be a laugh or a smile that indicated comprehension. The caring and love of staff members transcended linguistic barriers.

Focusing on Positive Outcomes

"Can you love them enough to help them learn?" is also an example of a question focused on positive outcomes. Another such question is "How can I help them to love each other?" This new question reminded me of the importance of providing models of collaboration. As a result, I expanded the consultation by bringing in a multiracial consultant team.

The facility was divided along lines of race, with white people in the management positions and people of color in service delivery positions. We believed that modeling interracial and intercultural collaboration in the consulting team would furnish an example with which different groups could identify. We also wanted to have people in charge who could be seen by service staff as representing them.

Our multiracial team consisted of the original Consultant, a Black woman, a white woman with a national reputation in the diversity consulting world, and a Latina woman whose training skills were known to draw in the most hardened participants.[6] This team made it possible for me to continue in a competent manner. Once the team was in place, one of the first things I noticed was how deskilled I had become in the process of working with the organization. So much time and energy had been spent trying to cope with my own feelings and trying to protect myself and other members of the organization there was little possibility of bringing forth the best that I could offer. I realized that, in contested terrains, the daily demands of survival in an oppressive society overshadow competence and stifle creativity.

Having new members join the consulting team allowed me to lift up my own thoughts and then help the members of the organization lift theirs. With colleagues on board to share the work, I was able to remember Ben Zander's idea, "Never doubt the capacity of the people you lead to accomplish whatever you dream for them." As in "possibility therapy" (O'Hanlon et al., 1999) focusing on positive outcomes gives the organization the opportunity to acknowledge its own experiences and to move toward positive growth and change.

Building Empathy and Respect

In the organization described, staff were engaged in conflict at the intergroup level. Blacks were in conflicts with whites. Managers were in conflict with service delivery staff and each group believed that their group alone had the interest of patients at heart. The Consultant's role was to create the context for a transformational conversation. Working toward dialogue in the multicultural change team, I now saw the possibility of creating the context for a transformational conversation. Building an empathic relationship with members of the staff who were respected by others in the organization was an important first step.

Empathy building, a fundamental aspect of loving, is both a task and a goal. Wells' instruction (1999) was to "engage in a deeply contactful relationship with the group." Each member of our consulting team took it as part of the work to build relationships with members of the agency team and other influential members in the organization.

This effort was confined at first to one-on-one conversations, where questions could be asked and doubts privately shared. We chose people for whom we could feel empathy and compassion, even if they had been at times antagonistic to the Initiative. We hoped that our ability to understand them and love them would bring forth their strengths. This effort is still in the beginning stages. Our next step will be to build some smaller intergroup conversations alongside the conversations of the Diversity Committee. We know from our own teaching and consulting that it is through interpersonal relationship that bias and antagonism are transcended.

One question that began to seem important was: how does an organization or group commonly define love? In its everyday work and everyday discourse, what word emerges on a regular basis that is most analogous to the word love or most closely reflects a loving stance? Remember the Haitian woman described earlier, the one who said, "Even the Bible said we should respect each other?" Over and over, service delivery staff focused on the word respect. When the staff felt mistreated, they would put it as: "we want respect." When I would speak of race or of racism, the staff would again say, "we must respect one another." When, in a Diversity Committee meeting, I named respect as the shared desire of staff members in the facility, heads around the table nodded in agreement. In the lexicon of this organization, respect was the reflection of love they desired to see. The word "respect" is becoming the mantra of the consulting team and we have begun to include it in our work with the organization so that our training package "Developing Strong Diverse Teams in the Workplace" is being redesigned as "Respect and Collaboration in the Workplace."

Holding the Group-as-a-Whole

The question "Can you help them . . . " requires multidimensional partiality (Nagy, 1973). The consultant is oriented toward being on everyone's side and seeing from everyone's perspective. She must work on behalf of everyone, which in Wells' socio-analytic systemic language is the group-as-a-whole. Taking sides with particular persons or groups risks setting off an escalating dynamic that worsens the situation that already exists.

Bringing a multiracial team into the organization was very instrumental in holding the group-as-a-whole. I was certainly guided by my philosophy and my training to hold the whole group, not parts of it. But the conflict in this organization, and the frequent attacks on me made it very hard to maintain a stance of multidimensional partiality in practice. The white consultant on our team helped by her willingness to step forward and work with staff members in a way they were not yet ready to have me do. The third member of our consulting team was a Latina woman and she completed our team in its reflection of the ethnic/racial diversity at the agency. As Jesse Jackson says, "Don't choose sides. Choose peace, and bring the sides together." Working with a multiracial/multiethnic team presents a model of collaboration that illustrates how powerful groups can be when they work together.

In this organization, what unites staff is their shared fear of downsizing, their concerns for future employment and their desire for respectful treatment in the workplace. Another way to hold the group is to focus on future employability. This has become another training agenda for the consulting team. Following Lynn Hoffman's communal perspective (in press), consultants who work with the group-as-a-whole must defy borders and build community at the most comprehensive level possible.

Black Love

Considering the question of love in the context of this consultation, I thought about the relevance of the idea of Black love. Wells was the founder of the Black Love workshops; a lifetime member of the national "Black Church"; a man devoted to The Word, especially as sung in spirituals and gospel music. As a person who believes deeply in the human family, would I be making my focus, too parochial or even potentially biased, by focusing on Black love?

In the end, I feel it is not possible to neglect consideration of what it means to do this work as a Black consultant, or what it means to love and work in the Black tradition. Love is a universal human emotion and action. Yet, as with every emotion and action, there are unique individual and cultural expressions. Black love is deeply rooted in the Christian tradition. Black love is the love of a people who go into the Lion's den and still survive. It is the love of a people who are oppressed and despised and who, nonetheless, intentionally hold on to loving.

Perhaps the most well known proponent of Black love was Martin Luther King, Jr. While in jail in 1957, King wrote his famous piece, "Loving your enemies." Beginning with Matthew 5:43-48,

> Ye have heard that it hath been said, Thou shalt love thy Neighbor, and hate thine enemy. But I say unto you, Love your enemies, bless them that curse you, do good to them that hate you, and pray for them which despitefully use you, and persecute you; that ye may be children of your Father which is in heaven.

King considers the "insistent questions and persistent objections" surrounding the idea of loving your enemies, and offers many positive responses. One idea that speaks strongly to me is Dr. King's statements that " . . . we must recognize that the evil deed of the enemy-neighbor, the thing that hurts never quite expresses all that he is" (p. 5). There is goodness alongside, outside the wrong that we, as human beings, all do.

Black writers Denene Millner and Nick Chiles (1999) believe that Black love is significant for its love of community, for it emphasis on community building as opposed to a sole focus on dyadic relationships. Black love is also notable for its emphasis on making "a joyful noise unto the Lord." I remember the praise and uplift of Leroy Wells's funeral service. Amid the grief and tears, and the Howard University flags flown at half-mast, was the celebration of life so typical of the Black Church. The congregation sang joyously the words of the hymn, "Excellent." "Excellent. My God is excellent. Excellent is his name" was a phrase that spoke for two that day, for the spirit of God that Wells called Father, and for one of his beloved sons, Leroy, carried back home at the age of forty-five. This joyful, spirit-filled, expression of the beloved community is what we call Black love.

A SUMMARY METAPHOR

The members of organizations are often like the "caracoles" (shells) one collects on a trip to the beach. In contested terrains, human beings are like the shattered and trashed shells found on a highly trafficked beach, destroyed by the explosion of human life around them. Like people who work in a hostile environment, these shells are crushed down, walked on, trampled.

The consultant searches for wholeness. There are other shells, like the ones found by setting out on a small boat with a tiny outboard motor on a day trip to an offshore island. On this quest, one can approach a pristine shoreline with a tiny stretch of sand. It is long and wide enough to beach the boat, to get out and stretch and swim and search for the "caracoles" in the clean, unsullied surf. The shells in that place can be gathered whole. Their multicolored blues, purples, pinks and browns, become luminescent in the ocean drops that cling to their rounded, curving surfaces. These shells, like questions entering into themselves, can reveal hidden treasure if we have the courage and the fortitude to keep moving inward.

This is the diversity the consultant seeks to locate and create–the fresh, multicolored, multishaped harmony that can be composed within a loving peaceful hand. A loving hand is like the larger shell in which the others can be nested; the varied types and shapes create interest and stimulation. This "holding" shell provides the context for centering, for gathering together the group-as-a-whole. In my vision, this is how love can transform the subject and the object, the consultant and the organization.

This paper has attempted to describe the labor of the heart for those consulting on contested terrain. What sustains the consultant is the wonder of the work, the awe and reverence for humanity, and the appreciation of the gift of love and wholeness waiting at the end. The personal gift to the consultant is the perfecting of the Self, using the powers of love and learning. She reaches as high as possible, as high as necessary, to create harmony in the contested terrain of organizational life.

NOTES

1. This idea was first presented to the author in a sermon by Reverend Ed Harding.
2. In some translations of the Bagavad Gita the word Self is used. Capitalized in its translation to English from the sankrit word *atman*, it conveys the inner reality, the spiritual principle, of a person who is inseparable from the whole of creation. It is not to be confused with the individuality of a person (ahakara).
3. This draws on Edward Said's use of the term "contested territories," which is the name he gives to countries who have been divided as a result of internal conflicts and the intrusion of hegemonic forces, e.g., India and Pakistan, North and South Korea, etc.
4. The Consultant in this case is the author.
5. This question was suggested to me by Sandra Nelson.
6. I am grateful to my team of fellow consultants, Rita Hardiman and Rosie Castañeda.

REFERENCES

Alderfer, C..(1998) "Papers of Leroy Wells, Jr.: Overview." *The Journal of Applied Behavioral Science,* Vol. 34, No. 4, 377-378.

Boszormenyi-Nagy, I., Sparks, G. (1984). *Invisible loyalties: Reciprocity in intergenerational family therapy.* New York: Brunner/Mazel.

Fleischman, P, R. (1989). *The healing zone: Religious issues in psychotherapy.* New York: Paragon House. (Title changed to *The Healing Spirit: Religious Issues in Psychotherapy.*)

de Shazer, S. (1994). *Words were originally magic.* New York: W.W. Norton.

Hoffman, L. (in press). "A Communal Perspective for Family Therapy."

Jones, L. B. (1995). *Jesus CEO: Using Ancient Wisdom for Visionary Leadership.* New York: Hyperion.

King, M. L. Loving your enemies. *Essay Series,* No. 1. Published by the A.J. Muste Memorial Institute.

Manz, C., Manz, K., Marx, R. & Neck, C. (in press). *Loving and Leading with the Wisdom of Solomon.* San Francisco: Berrett-Koehler.

Miller, B. S. (trans.). (1986). *The Bhagavad-Gita: Krishna's Counsel in Time of War.* New York: Bantam Books.

Millner, D. & Chiles, N. (1999). *What brothers think, What sistahs know: The truth about Black love and relationships.* Quill.

O'Hanlon, W. H., Beadle, S. O'Hanlon, B. (1999). *A guide to possibility land: Fifty-one methods for doing brief respectful therapy.* New York: W.W. Norton.

O'Rourke. C. (1997). "Listening for the sacred: Addressing spiritual issues in the group treatment of adults with mental illness." *Smith College Studies in Social Work,* 67 (2), March 1997.

Quinn, Robert E. (1996). *Deep change: Discovering the leader within.* San Francico: Jossey-Bass Publishers.

Romney, P., Tatum, T., & Jones, J. (1992) "Feminist Strategies for Teaching About Oppression: The importance of process." *Women's Studies Quarterly,* 1992. Vol. XX; Nos. 1&2, pp. 95-110.

Wells, L., Jr. (1980). "The Group-as-whole: A Systemic Socio-Analytic Perspective on Interpersonal and Group Relations." In C. P. Alderfer & C. L. Cooper (Eds.), *Advances in social experiential processes,* Volume 2. London: John Wiley & Sons Ltd.

Wells. L., Jr. (1999). (Ed. K. Smith) Consultants as Nautical Navigators: A Metaphor for Group-Takers. *The Journal of Applied Behavior Science,* Vol. 34, No 4 December 1998, 379-391.

White, M. (1995*). Re-Authoring Lives.* Adelaide, S.A.: Dulwich Centre Publications.

The Talking Oppression Blues: Including the Experience of Power/Powerlessness in the Teaching of "Cultural Sensitivity"

N. Norma Akamatsu

This chapter focuses on a fundamental problem in the teaching of clinical practice across race and cultural difference: how to develop greater attunement to and facility in talking about power and the experience of inequality, especially among those in positions of privilege.[1] As I have listened to people of color and white people talking together about race, ethnicity and culture, the conversation frequently diverges around the phenomenon of power (hooks, 1995; Pinderhughes, 1989; Sue & Sue, 1990).[2] Power differences are less apparent to the privileged, who can more readily accept a view of American society as classless and color-blind–the myth of "the level playing field." Such a view, however, ignores the unrelenting experience of inferior status, economic discrimination, marginalization and injustice that many people of color and other oppressed groups encounter. The resulting social disparities can become brutally salient to some, while remaining veiled to those who are protected. The depth and breadth of this split in experience are captured in the title of one study on race relations: *Two Nations: Black and White, Separate, Hostile, Unequal* (Hacker, 1992).

N. Norma Akamatsu, MSW, is in private practice in Northampton, MA and is Adjunct Faculty at the Smith College School for Social Work.

Address correspondence to: N. Norma Akamatsu, Northampton Institute for Family Therapy, 151 Main Street, Northampton, MA 01060.

Reprinted with permission from Re-visioning Family Therapy: Race, Culture, and Gender in Clinical Practice, edited by Monica McGoldrick. Copyright 1998 by Guilford Publications, Inc., 72 Spring Street, New York NY 10012.

[Haworth co-indexing entry note]: "The Talking Oppression Blues: Including the Experience of Power/Powerlessness in the Teaching of 'Cultural Sensitivity.'" Akamatsu, N. Norma. Co-published simultaneously in *Journal of Feminist Family Therapy* (The Haworth Press, Inc.) Vol. 11, No. 4, 2000, pp. 83-97; and: *Feminism, Community, and Communication* (ed: Mary E. Olson) The Haworth Press, Inc., 2000, pp. 83-97.

When power differences are not addressed, the "two nations" remain irreparably disconnected. This was apparent in one project, for example, as a painful contrast emerged between White and Black college students.[3] In discussing stereotypes, a White woman argued energetically against "putting people into categories," insisting, "I want to be judged as an individual, not as apart of any group–which is exactly the way I relate to all other people, too!" Her friend told the story of two preschoolers, Black and White, examining their skin tones. The White child affirmed, "You know, we're the same on the inside." The extent to which such idealism falls flat for people of color–the privilege inherent in assuming that one can choose not to be racially categorized or can claim their common humanity–was not apparent until Black students responded. A young man used these measured words:

> If we're not born racist, what happens along the way? The real question is–does their *teacher* think those children are the same inside? I'm glad these White people say they are not prejudiced, but they're not running the government and stereotypes are not the problem. It's when you have the ability to restrict me because of your prejudice. It all comes down to power.

Phrases like "multiculturalism" and "cultural difference" often obscure the linking of "different" and "less" in our society. This inattention to the experience of inequality can nullify attempts at "cultural sensitivity." "Not having to notice" is a privilege and noticing, not surprisingly, arouses much anxiety and defensiveness.

McGoldrick's (1994) account of the halting expansion of her own awareness is a candid illustration of the varying ability to perceive power, depending on one's own position:

> Over the years, I have been mystified by the reactivity of men to [feminist] issues. . . . Longtime male colleagues came up to me and said, " . . . Why are you so angry at men? Did you hate your father? . . . I'm not sexist. I've never mistreated a woman, so why are you blaming me for all this? Why are you saying we have the power? I feel quite powerless. We men have problems too, you know. After all, we're not allowed to feel." (p. 42)

> Within the past few years, I began to be confronted with race and racism and now it was "I" who was on the other side of the power imbalance. Suddenly, I wanted to say to others the same things men had been saying to me: "Why are you so angry? . . . I have nothing to do with racism, slavery or segregation. I've never mistreated a person of color. I would love to change things, but I don't have the power, either. White people have experienced oppression, too–let me tell you about it." (p. 42)

Romney (in Romney, Tatum, & Jones, 1992), from her vantage point as an African American professor, writes:

> ... I am always struggling as a teacher who is a member of a targeted racial group to understand the experiences of whites when they confront their own racism. In the last Psychology of Oppression class I taught, I shared ... that I could not fully understand why white students found it so upsetting to be called a racist. I explained that from an African-American perspective my thinking is that, of course, white people are racist. Racism is embodied in the culture.... Both I and the students of color in class began to understand that the term racism evokes for many whites an all-or-nothing feeling ... (p. 103)

A bi-racial team of anti-bias educators (Ayvazian and Tatum, 1996) summarizes the situation:

> Many people of color understand the power differential inherent in the three manifestations of racism: personal, cultural, and institutional. They view racism not as an individual issue but as a systemic problem. However, many white people still characterize racism as a virulent form of individual prejudice–they reduce the problem to ... "individual acts of meanness." They are unschooled in the systematic ways that racism has been institutionalized and are oblivious to the reality of privilege given automatically and invisibly to white people every single day. (p. 18)

"RACISM 101": FIRST LESSONS

Because of the embeddedness of racism, white skin privilege is a camouflage for those who are not targeted. Not perceiving themselves as unknowing, they may never think, or may feel vaguely reluctant, to ask for information. In teaching, my colleague and I have found it most useful to begin with specific content describing how "invisible" power discrepancies operate.

Differentiating personal, institutional, and cultural racism is a crucial starting point. In our course, these distinctions are explained and clarified in the first class to prepare for that day's assignment: Students are sent in pairs to roam the surrounding New England town to compile a list of 20 examples of cultural racism, defined as "any message or image prevalent in society that promotes the false but constant idea that White is the standard, ideal, normal." Computer ads, monuments, magazine covers, greeting cards, museum portraits, cosmetics, baby products, and children's toys that only portray White people are frequently cited. The subtext of "White is intelligent, White is heroic, White is successful, White is beautiful, White is hygienic, White is cute" is boldly highlighted. Like a rap on the head from a Zen master, this exercise awakens White students to the pervasive ordinariness of a now-blatant cultural racism.

Basic information about systematic forms of contemporary racism, more subtle than the legal segregation of the past, is also presented at the outset. Some examples are discriminatory banking and real estate practices, or the corporate "glass ceilings" that limit promotion of peoples of color. Racism in educational systems and the considerable impact of attitudinal differences are also noted. Citing research that shows relatively depressed levels of achievement among African American students (including middle-class youngsters), the psychologist Claude Steele (1992) hypothesizes a process of disidentification from educational institutions. He attributes this to the power of negative expectations, an impact long considered in our field:

> Terms like "prejudice" and "racism" often miss the full scope of racial devaluation in our society . . . in all of us, not just in the strongly prejudiced . . . even in blacks themselves. . . . Sooner or later it forces on its victims [the] painful realization . . . that society is preconditioned to see the worst in them. (pp. 72-74)

Finally, we invite students to use the Multicultural Organizational Assessment Inventory (Jackson & Holvino, 1988), which outlines differing types of organizational response to racism, examine work contexts. The impact of exclusionary organizations (e.g., the Ku Klux Klan or country clubs) pales in comparison to the far-reaching effects of organizations with an attitude of passive compliance: "We meet all equal-opportunity criteria. Our doors are open, but 'they' don't apply!" The need for active restructuring and systemic change goes unrecognized. As an African American diversity trainer succinctly observes, "I'm less afraid of the men in white sheets than the men in blue suits" (Kenneth Jones, personal communication, June 1996).

RACISM AS DOMINANT DISCOURSE

Many White students begin to experience an uneasy puzzlement over their previous inability to notice these immense and pervasive systems of inequity. The framework of "dominant discourses," used by narrative therapists (e.g., Hare-Mustin, 1994; White & Epston, 1990; White, 1993), provides a theoretical perspective that makes sense of their predicament. Based on social constructionist principles, this perspective questions what we ordinarily regard as "neutral," "objective," or "common-sense" and reaches for the underlying values embedded within cultural norms. This analysis redirects our attention to the specific historical, social, economic, and political contexts that shape (and are in turn supported by) culturally approved beliefs. The subtle endorsement of particular arrangements of privilege and power is an especially important implication. For example, a Latino family therapist complained about a national family therapy conference brochure. The series of photographs of featured clinicians included only White people. This was met by the shocked dismay of a White colleague, who realized she hadn't even noticed the omission of people of color. The biases embedded within the dominant discourse are hidden by their very ordinariness, and this sense of "normality" functions to preclude questioning (White, 1993). "You first have to realize you're blind before you can try to see" (M. Pakman, personal communication, June 1995).

Previously applied to the problem of sexism (e.g., Weingarten, 1995), the construct of dominant discourses can be extended to the phenomenon of racism to investigate how unrecognized cultural assumptions inevitably envelop our clinical theory and practice. Deconstructive inquiry, a critical scrutiny of our own "taken-for-granted realities and practices" (White, 1993, p. 34), draws attention both to the shaping influence of larger social contexts and to the underlying values and biases that are enacted in therapy. The pedagogical efforts that accompany such an inquiry attempt to create a wedge of awareness that can help students "stand outside" of their accustomed views.

PUTTING THE WORLD BACK INTO THERAPY

A family therapist once proudly described her approach to a racially and ethnically diverse caseload: "I treat them all the same." Much of our theory has shared this bias, which universalizes the experience and social context of the White middle class. By contrast, a social constructionist perspective reiterates the fundamental and long-standing position taken by family therapists, especially those who have worked with oppressed populations: the absolute necessity of taking into account, and including in the therapeutic conversation, the impact of larger systems (see, e.g., Auerswald, 1968; Boyd-Franklin, 1989; Crawford, 1988; Goldner, 1985; Waldegrave, 1990). We ask students to consider the "mental health" implications of contingencies such as these:

- What if the family runs out of money for food by the third week of the month?
- What if a lesbian couple is raising a 14-year-old son in middle America?
- What if in one heterosexual couple, the man earns $65,000 and the woman earns $17,000?

- What if in another, the woman has a civil service position and the man can no longer find a job in the manufacturing industries that used to employ him?
- What if a 17-year-old Latino has no viable strategy for ever earning more than $12,000/year?
- What if a 9-year-old is the only African American girl in her elementary school?

We then consider the implications of locating the effects of these problems *within* people rather than taking broader social problems into account.[4]

WHITE IS HEALTHY: EUROCENTRIC THEORY

One student's list of cultural racism examples included these entries: "Band-Aids, Barbies, our theories" and was used to inaugurate a renewed appraisal of theory. Although initially very difficult for students to perceive, cultural biases are gradually discerned. Students make a start by recalling feminist critiques of psychological theory, with which they are usually more familiar, transposing from gender bias to cultural bias. Foucault's insight (cited by White & Epston, 1990) that power relations are embedded in and maintained by bodies of knowledge forms the basis of the critique. This analysis cast a more menacing light on clinical theory and stimulates a renewed analysis of the political impact of ideas. In this way, the implicit endorsement of Eurocentric communicational styles, ways of handling emotion, and nonverbal behaviors, as well as the Eurocentric focus on the individual and on heterosexual, two-parent family structures, becomes apparent. (For fuller accounts of such bias, see other chapters of this book; Falicov, 1995; and Hardy & Laszloffy, 1994.)

Awareness of the Eurocentric tendency toward "you-have-ethnicity-and-I-don't" attitudes (M. White, personal communication, July 1994) also promotes a more critical perspective on ethnic differences (McGoldrick, Giordano, & Pierce, 1996). A deconstructive inquiry can move beyond a one-sided description of "them" and toward a recursive dialogue, in which the student's own cultural and professional assumptions are also called into self-awareness and questioned.

Students are encouraged to become "transparent" (White, 1993)–that is, to make explicit how their clinical ideas and practices are linked to particular meaningful personal experiences, values, cultural contexts. They can invite their clients to do the same. For example, these questions can be used to engage immigrant mothers and their daughters in a conjoint deconstruction of their differing cultural premises about gender role (Akamatsu, 1995):

- What is the traditional role for women in your culture, as you understood that in your particular family?
- What was the impact of immigration or living in the United States on the traditional role?
- What aspects of the traditional role have the women in your family followed and what have they not followed, based on what experiences?
- Do you see yourself as similar to or different from your daughter/mother in this regard?

LOCAL KNOWLEDGE

The deeply entrenched tendency to ignore, disqualify, or pathologize the experience of targeted peoples requires our energetic attention and ingenuity to redress.[5] Various opportunities for recognizing local, "nonexpert" ways of knowing and problem solving can be considered: for example, the structural family therapy technique termed the "search for strengths." More specifically, acts of resistance can be identified and validated; the resilience required to manage oppression can be acknowledged; and the ethical implications of this struggle can be identified ("What does your tenacity say about what you are really committed to in your life?") (see Walsh, Chapter 5, and Hines, Chapter 6, this volume; White, 1993).

Therapists and teams can transform themselves into what L. Hoffman (personal communication, 1995) calls an "honoring community"-one that bears witness both to the painful realities of clients oppressive situations and to the strengths that clients show, including the adaptive value of behavior that might easily be labeled "problematic" if the demands or influence of the social context are ignored. Ayvazian and Tatum's (1996) "radical prescription" for developing more understanding about the experience of oppression is quite straightforward: "Listen and believe" (p. 18). They continue:

> Whites need to listen to the stories and struggles of people of color in their own or surrounding communities. Not judge, debate, defend, solve, or critique-but listen. Through the simple act of listening, the subtle and pervasive nature of "neoracism" . . . may become evident.
>
> However, listening itself will not reach hearts or change minds unless white people are encouraged to take another step that contradicts countless messages from their growing years, that is: to believe people of color. (p. 18)

Students or faculty members of color can offer their personal experience or critical feedback as a way to expand others' sensitivity to an unfamiliar existential territory. However, a recurring problem is that the burden of teaching is habitually placed on the oppressed; this often exacerbates the lack of initiative taken by those in power. Furthermore, discussing the impact of a subjugated status with people in a position of dominance is an inherently distressing step that renders a person immensely vulnerable. A student of color protested to us, "I am tired of being 'The Experience' for White students." Ayvazian and Tatum (1996) emphasize that people of color must feel such activities benefit them, and that clear guidelines and structures must be developed to safeguard the conversations. In the absence of such direct reports, there are many useful books, films and videos that relate quite powerfully the experiences of oppressed people.[6]

There are other important reasons why it may be better to postpone face-to-face dialogue until after some work is done independently by each group. Those in the targeted group may simply wish to have the freedom to focus on their own needs and agendas first. For those in the dominant group, apprehending their own privilege–the benefits automatically bestowed, embraced, and relied upon–can be an identity-shifting awakening. It has been aptly labeled a "disintegration experience" (Helms, 1990), more complicated in racially combined groups, and often greatly discomforting for people of color to witness.

STANDING OUTSIDE ONESELF

Self-reflexiveness can be encouraged in those in a position of dominance, even in the absence of such dialogue. Taking the role of "emissaries," they can attempt to listen through the lens of a particular oppressed group for the relevance of theory and appropriateness of practice. Such a re-visioning has proved invaluable, for example, in discussing "family life cycle" frameworks which tend to institutionalize the "Ozzie and Harriet" ideal. The family experiences of gay men and lesbians, people of color, various ethnic groups, single parents, and childless couples have gained more prominence through the use of this device. Another very important aspect of this reflexivity is considering how members of dominant groups may themselves be perceived–"imagining others imagining you."[7] This is an exercise in subject-object reversals, in which seeing the "self" as "other" may facilitate seeing the "other" as "self." This imagining also tends to expose more of the "invisible" mantle of privilege. Some of the questions raised are as follows:

- Considering specifically how you look, talk, dress, and so on, what stereotypes do you think people of color might hold about you?

- How might clients of color experience a predominantly White agency?
- How might social workers of color feel in these contexts?
- What might be useful in a dialogue between a White social worker and a client of color? That is, what do you imagine needs to be heard/experienced by this client in order to break the stereotypes?[8]

"MULTIPLEXITY"

In the process of teaching, these ideas and discussions help White students develop more awareness and knowledge. But managing their guilt or defensiveness about the advantages they enjoy involves articulation of other social constructionist principles, most basically the notion of multiple social identities. Falicov (1995) uses the term "ecological niche" to refer to the highly particular "combination of multiple contexts and partial cultural locations" an individual or family may occupy, "where views and values are shaped and where power or powerlessness are experienced" (pp. 376-377).

Theories of racial identity development for Whites and people of color (e.g., Helms, 1990; Tatum, 1992) are helpful, highlighting the relativity and context-dependent nature of our experience of our own race. Inevitable collisions, can be analyzed and demystified, such as the mismatch between a student of color invested in networking with other people of color and a White student anxious to forge cross-race connections.

One of the most important implications of our multiple social identities is the "multiplexity"[9]-that we may be disadvantaged in some contexts, yet privileged in others.

> In each form of oppression, there is a dominant group (the one that receives the unearned advantage, benefit, or privilege) and a targeted group (that is denied . . .). We know the litany of dominants: white people, males, Christians, heterosexuals, able-bodied people, those in their middle years and those who are middle or upper class. . . .
> We also know that everyone has multiple social identities-we are all dominant and targeted simultaneously. I am, in the very same moment, dominant as a white person and targeted as a woman. (Ayvazian, 1995, p. 17)

However, the underlying duality-the coexistence of one's own privileged and targeted positions-is not easy to apprehend emotionally. It requires a more complex view of identity, in which contradictory experiences of advantage and disadvantage form ragged layers. This demands a particular sort of "both-and" holding that relies on the ability to "contain opposites."

The [both-and] metaphor embodies an intellectual, political and psychological ideal: the attempt to recognize the value of competing and contradictory perspectives and to tolerate the psychological experience of extreme ambivalence without splitting ideas and people into good and bad. (Goldner, 1992, pp. 56-57)

Foucault's perception (cited by White & Epston, 1990) that dominant discourses constrain both privileged and targeted groups can facilitate this understanding. I have reminded White students that they did *not,* upon turning age 21, march into City Hall and ask to sign up for "White skin privilege" to gain access to benefits systematically at the lifelong expense of peoples of color. This defines cultural racism as colonizing the minds of both people of color and Whites, who are inducted into their respective albeit vastly different positions.

LIVED EXPERIENCE

I have found that one of the most useful ways to approach these complicated issue of multiple social identities is through telling my personal story as a third-generation Japanese American. I have likened my growing-up experience to a checkerboard of disadvantage and privilege. Like a character in a Victorian novel, I was catapulted from "pauper" to "prince." I was one of the poorest kids, and one of the very few children of color, in an elementary school of predominantly well-to-do white children. From there, I went on to Booker T. Washington, Public Junior High School 54, where I was conspicuously advantaged as one of the most economically secure youngsters in a predominantly Black and Puerto Rican student body, with a high proportion of families supported by welfare. I first developed consciousness of race amid the still lingering anti-Japanese stereotypes of World War II; I came into adulthood during the Vietnam War years of "gooks" and "dinks"; and, in between, I was identified as a member of a "model minority." I tell the story of a road trip to the South in 1957, in which my then 11-year-old brother needed to make an emergency bathroom stop. My father pulled up to a roadside diner, where Johnny raced to the restrooms in the back, only to come careening out front to the car again: "The bathrooms have signs. One says 'White.' The other says 'Colored.' Where am I supposed to go?" And without skipping a beat, my mother told him firmly: "White. White. You go to the White bathroom."

This anecdote has come to symbolize my sense of participation in privilege. When I imagine how other people of color (people of other colors) might look at me, I would guess that despite its hazards, the social access conceded to Asians in this society is perceived as a "relative privilege."[10] Acknowledging the advantages that I can recognize in my life has eased my conversations with people of other targeted groups. A student pointed out, very importantly, how this acknowledgment simultaneously recognizes another's oppression and becomes an important form of validation.

THE PROBLEM OF COMPETING "-ISMS"

As political and economic forces increasingly threaten to divide and conquer some of us more than others, our connections become vital and tenuous. Our sense of oppression is a double-edged sword. The marginalization we have experienced, when unacknowledged, can polarize and divide us. Given a dominant discourse of "equality," these experiences are typically suppressed, so that we are all starved for validation. But the need for acknowledgment of the particular injustices we have endured can drive us into a symmetrical, mutually isolating competition to be heard. At the same time, these experiences, although different and unique, can provide a basis for coalition and a connecting arc/ark of mutual recognition when they are told, heard, and believed. Over time, collectively, we will have to learn to balance our need for validation with acknowledgment of our privilege and a readiness to validate another's suffering. A defensive holding on to our sense of disadvantage is likely to be experienced as denial of another's oppression. Ironically, we may only be released from our defensive posture by another's acknowledgment of our pain.

For their final assignment in our course students are asked to inventory the dominant and targeted positions they occupy (in relation to racism, sexism, classism, heterosexism, anti-Semitism, abilism, and ageism), and to write something about "what personal experiences have brought the issue of racism to life for you." This formalizes an ongoing process, apparent in their journals, of connecting with the emotional truth of racial oppression through their own experiences of marginalization (of feeling "less than" or blocked by powerful social forces)–as women, members of the working class, gays or lesbians, Jews, differently abled persons and/or survivors of familial abuse.[11] The "both-and" process of journal-writing about these or other more idiosyncratic experiences, while increasing the awareness of privilege, is pivotal in the educational process. This exercise also addresses the confusion of those who enjoy a broad array of advantages. A heterosexual White male student noted his "triple dominance" with abashment, anxious that he had no basis for claiming an emotional connection to the experience of disadvantage. However, even as he developed an accounting of his privilege, he was able to identify areas of private suffering that constituted a personally meaningful basis for empathy, as well as those important in developing his commitment as a White anti-racist activist. Acknowledgment in the form of detailed and attentive written responses by both coteachers, who constituted a small "honoring community" for the students, further supported this development.

CONCLUSION

Some months after completing our class on racism, a student's letter was published in her local newspaper, registering her distress at the mistaken arrest of an African American woman on shoplifting charges:

> There's no way around it. If you grew up in this country you absorbed negative information about anyone who was not white. You were also fed negative information about anyone who was gay, lesbian, bisexual, overweight, old, with a physical or mental challenge, poor, or even female. No this is not your fault. You didn't ask to be born into this. But you were. If you're white, you might feel racism affects you, and it does; psychologically, spiritually, emotionally . . . but it's not the same as the daily grinding experience for people of color, who are systematically oppressed.
>
> The responsibility to dismantle racism and every other "-ism" belongs to each and every one of us.
>
> Passionately,
> Anna Gailitis

As practitioners/teachers who occupy positions of privilege and who choose to confront racism, we must stand ready to initiate dialogue about power and to demonstrate that we possess the "ears" that can hear these concerns. As we continue to learn more and talk together more openly about the lived experiences of privilege and oppression, teaching situations and the practice of therapy offer possible new sites of awakening, resistance, coalition, and connection.

NOTES

1. This discussion is oriented to the teaching of White students, with whom I shared a unique learning experience. To educate myself more, I began coteaching a required racism course at the Smith College School for Social Work in 1995. Due to a student initiative to permit students of color to be grouped together, my sections have consisted exclusively of White students. I developed the "clinical applications" portion of a course designed by my coteacher, Andrea Ayvazian, PhD, whom I wish

to acknowledge and thank for her inestimable contribution to the work discussed here.

2. Lee Mun Wah's video documentary *The Color of Fear* (1994), about an interracial dialogue among eight men, is a vivid and trenchant demonstration of this problem.

3. These perspectives were voiced by African American, Jewish, and white non-Jewish students as part of a project on "Black/Jewish/Other" Relations, organized by the Office of Human Relations, University of Massachusetts–Amherst, in 1995. A conversation was constructed through the exchange of videotaped discussions among homogeneous groups.

4. These questions were suggested by the work of Carter (1988), Crawford (1988), Waldgrave (1990), and White and Epston (1990).

5. We have used M. White's (personal communication, 1994) "Conscious Purpose and Commitment Exercise" which provides students with a direct experience of the contrast between a pathologizing description and a deconstructive inquiry. In this exercise, negative ascriptions about their choice of profession are recalled and then a brief history of actual experiences and ethical decisions is elicited that is acknowledging of the values and personal meaning inherent in their choice of profession.

6. The video *True Colors* (Lukasiewicz & Harvey, 1991) is one example. A white and an African-American man posed man posed as new arrivals to a midwestern city and were secretly videotaped while searching for jobs, flagging taxis, hunting for apartments, shopping for cars, and so on. The chasm separating the "two nations" is conveyed with stunning immediacy by the literally split-screen portrayal of their unequal experiences, offering a unique basis for comparison and double description.

7. E. H. Auerswald introduced me to this approach in his design for a crosscultural dailogue process among ethnically diverse high school students, which I facilitated in Hawaii in 1976. His idea of exchanging videotaped discussions among homogeneous groups was replicated in my later work with college students at the University of Massachusetts–Amherst.

8. A telling piece of feedback was student concern that these efforts would not be supported in the workplace. At the close of our 5-week course, students felt they were now significantly more cognizant of the impact of racism than most supervisors they would encounter.

9. Cornel West's phrase, employed during a dialogue on Black-Jewish relations with Michael Lerner, October 1995, Mount Holyoke College, South Hadley, MA.

10. This is not intended to discount the reality of anti-Asian discriminatory attitudes. Chang (1995), for example, points out how the "model minority myth . . . renders the oppression of Asian Americans invisible" (p. 328).

11. Grillo and Wildman (1995) note the danger of presuming to understand one sort of oppression through personal experience with another. However, there is a subtle but significant difference between an uncritical substitution and the coming to life of another's experience through reference to one's own.

REFERENCES

Akamatsu, N. (1995). The defiant daughter and compliant mother: Multicultural dialogues on woman's role. *In Session: Psychotherapy in Practice*, 1: 43-55.

Auerswald, E.H. (1968) Interdisciplinary versus ecological approach. *Family Process,* 7: 202-215.

Ayvazian, A. (1995). Interrupting the cycle of oppression: The Role of allies as agents of change. *Smith College School for Social Work Journal*, 13: 17-20.

Ayvazian, A. and Tatum, B. (1996, January-February). Can we talk? *Sojourners*, pp. 16-19.

Boyd-Franklin, N. (1989). *Black families in therapy: A Multisystems Approach.* New York: Guilford Press.

Carter, B. (1988). The person who has the gold makes the rules. In M. Walters, B. Carter, P. Papp, & O. Silverstein, *The invisible web: Gender patterns in family relationships.* New York: Guilford Press.

Chang, R. (1995). Toward an Asian American Legal Scholarship. In R. Delgado (Ed.), *Critical Race Theory: The Cutting Edge.* Philadelphia: Temple University Press.

Crawford, S. (1988). Cultural context as a factor in the expansion of therapeutic conversation with lesbian families. *Journal of Strategic and Systemic Therapies*, 7 (3): 2-10.

Falicov, C. (1995). Training to think culturally: A Multidimensional comparative framework. *Family Process,* 34 (4): 373-388.

Goldner, V. (1985). Feminism and family therapy. *Family Process,* 24: 31-47.

Goldner, V. (1992). Making room for both-and. *Family Therapy Networker,* 16: 54-61.

Grillo, T. & Wildman, S. (1995). Obscuring the importance of race: The Implication of making comparisons between racism and sexism (or other -isms). In R. Delgado (Ed.), *op.cit.*

Hacker, A. (1992). *Two nations, Black and White, separate, hostile, unequal.* New York: Scribner.

Hardy, K. & Laszloffy, T. (1994). Deconstructing race in family therapy. In R. Almeida,(Ed.) *Expansions of Feminist Family Theory Through Diversity.* New York: The Haworth Press, Inc.

Hare-Mustin, R. (1994). Discourses in the mirrored room: A postmodern analysis of therapy. In *Family Process,* 33 (1): 19-35.

Helms, J. (Ed.)(1990). *Black and White Racial Identity: Theory, Research and Practice.* Westport, CT: Greenwood Press.

hooks, b. (1995). *Killing rage/ending racism.* New York: Holt.

Jackson, B. and Holvino, E. (April, 1988). Developing multicultural organizations. In *Journal of Applied Behavioral Science and Religion,* pp. 14-19.

Lukasiewicz, M. & Harvey, E. (Producers). (1991). *True Colors* [video]. (Available from MTI/Film & Video, 420 Academy Dr., Northbrook, IL 60062.

McGoldrick, M. (1994). The Ache for home. *Family Therapy Networker,* 18: 38-45.

McGoldrick, M., Giordano, J. & Pearce, J. (1996). *Ethnicity and family therapy.* (Eds.) New York: Guilford Press.

Lee Mun Wah (Producer). (1994). *The color of fear* [video]. (Available from Stir Fry Productions, 470 Third St., Oakland, CA. 94607.)

Pinderhughes, E. (1989). *Understanding race, ethnicity and power: The key to efficacy in clinical practice.* New York: Free Press.

Romney, P., Tatum, B. & Jones, J. (1992). Feminist strategies for teachng about opression: The importance of process. *Women's Studies Quarterly,* 20: 95-110.

Steele, C. (1992). Race and the schooling of Black Americans. *The Atlantic Monthly,* April, pp.68-78.

Sue, D. W. and Sue, D. (1990). *Counseling the culturally different: Theory and practice.* New York: Wiley.

Tatum, B. (1992). Talking about race, learning about racism: The application of racial identity development theory in the classroom. *Harvard Educational Review,* 62 (1): 1-23.

Waldegrave, C. (1990). Just therapy. Social justice in family therapy. *Dulwich Centre Newsletter,* 1, 21-27.

Weingarten, K. (1995). Radical listening: Challenging cultural beliefs for and about mothers. *Journal of Feminist Family Therapy,* 7 (1/2): 7-22.

White, M. (1993). Deconstruction and therapy. In S. Gilligan and R. Price (Eds.) *Therapeutic Conversations.* New York: Norton.

White, M. & Epston, D. (1990). *Narrative means to therapeutic ends.* New York: Norton.

Theorizing Culture: Narrative Ideas and Practice Principles

Joan Laird

"Cultural diversity," "multiculturalism," "culturally sensitive practice," "cultural competence"-these have become the buzz phrases of the 1990s in the mental health professions. But the term "culture" covers a territory that contains vast possibilities for understanding and interpretation. We use words like "culture," "gender," " race," "ethnicity," "social class," or "sexual orientation" as if they had consistent definitions and as if we had some agreement on their meanings.

As mental health practitioners, we are repeatedly exhorted to become culturally competent and to practice ethnic-sensitive practice. This usually means educating ourselves about the characteristics of the "other," and discovering what the study of a group of people-with origins different from our own, from another nation, with another skin color, with different genitalia, with same-sex life partners-can tell us about ourselves. To learn about the other, said anthropologists, was to learn about us. As Bateson (1979) put it, "it takes two somethings to create a difference" (p. 68). Thus, you may know you are French because someone else is Swedish; I know I am short (in this context) because you are tall. In Western culture, at least, we've organized ourselves around "difference" and particularly around binary oppositions-male-female, black-white, gay-straight, rich-poor. To be culturally competent has meant, then, to know about and to appreciate "difference." But "differ-

---

Joan Laird, MS, LICSW, is Professor Emerita, Smith College School for Social Work.

Reprinted with permission from *Re-visioning Family Therapy: Race, Culture, and Gender in Clinical Practice*, edited by Monica McGoldrick. Copyright 1998 by Guilford Publications, Inc., 72 Spring Street, New York, NY 10012.

[Haworth co-indexing entry note]: "Theorizing Culture: Narrative Ideas and Practice Principles." Laird, Joan. Co-published simultaneously in *Journal of Feminist Family Therapy* (The Haworth Press, Inc.) Vol. 11, No. 4, 2000, pp. 99-114; and: *Feminism, Community, and Communication* (ed: Mary E. Olson) The Haworth Press, Inc., 2000, pp. 99-114.

ent from" often means "less than." Are there any other ways to think about thinking about culture?

"Culture" is a vast interdisciplinary topic that has generated floods of literature and research in the social sciences in the last decade, as well as central discussions in academia, in organizations, within the popular culture, and, of course, at professional conferences. How do we move beyond the cliché-ridden, often meaningless or undefined ways these notions are tacked on to diagnostic and other clinical languages, receiving little more than honorable mention? How do we surface our own cultural stories, our cultural identities? And, when it is important–as it almost always is–how do we locate the cultural stories and meanings of the people with whom we work?

My purpose in this chapter is to offer a number of ideas or metaphors that might be useful for thinking about how to think about "culture," and, using those ideas, to generate some principles for practice. These ideas are inspired by work from many directions, among them the postmodern movement, the interdisciplinary movement, the feminist critique, voices from various margins, and new work on gender and sexuality. I intend for these ideas to apply to any of the cultural categorizations we make in identifying and characterizing each other and in labeling various social groupings–categorizations such as gender, race, ethnicity, social class, or sexuality. These categorizations, these self-representations, are overlapping and simultaneous; we can "theorize" them using common points of reference.

THE NEED TO MOVE BEYOND STATIC NOTIONS OF CULTURE

Many clinicians believe these dimensions of human experience are vitally important, but have very different ideas about the meanings of these cultural categorizations and how they should be thought about in practice. In the ethnicity area, for example, some clinicians have argued that culture is "camouflage" (Friedman, 1980); that is, it is used in families in manipulative or controlling ways as a red herring, in order to preserve the status quo, bind children to their parents, keep family boundaries closed, and so on. Others, like Montalvo and Gutierrez (1983), have seen culture or ethnicity as a potential "mask" that can obscure people's problem-solving modes:

> By using cultural constraints selectively . . . the family can pull the therapist away from reality. The therapist is made to deal instead with a cultural image of the ethnic group. In the process the family–as simply people having difficulties in solving problems–is lost. (p. 16)

These authors have believed that if one is simply a good listener, or, as in the case of various family therapies, able to surface the family structure, rules, and other patterns, what is important about culture will emerge. One needs no special knowledge.

McGoldrick (1994), perhaps the most articulate and dedicated spokesperson in the clinical arena for the importance of the cultural dimension in family life, has taken a very different position. She points out that "ethnicity patterns our thinking, feeling and behavior in both obvious and subtle ways, playing a major role in determining what we eat, how we work, how we relate, how we celebrate holidays and ritual, and how we feel about life, death, and illness" (p. 335). In McGoldrick's view, although to learn about ethnic group practices and beliefs is to risk stereotyping, to pretend that there are no patterns is to mystify and disqualify human experience and to "perpetuate negative stereotyping" (p. 335).

Falicov (1995), in one kind of effort to avoid the risks of stereotyping, advocates what she calls a "multidimensional, comparative" training framework. "Culture is viewed as occurring in multiple contexts that create common 'cultural borderlands' as well as diversity; unpredictability and possibility, as well as regularity and constraint" (p. 373). She uses what she terms "basic parameters" common to all families–parameters such as ecological niche, migration patterns, degrees of acculturation, or life cycle events–to think comparatively. I see this effort, in part, as one of learning about how diverse people approach common human experiences rather than about ethnic groups or entities. It is one way of shifting the center and avoiding the "different from/less than" trap that comes from always beginning with the dominant experience.

My own view both combines and is somewhat different from any of these positions. I agree with McGoldrick about the power of culture and ethnicity (and gender, sexuality, social class, etc.) in shaping the self and the human story, and about how important it is for clinicians to learn how to access these stories. If we are to unpack cultural stories, we need to know enough to ask good questions, to "notice" culture in its many guises. I also believe, unlike Montalvo or Friedman, that whatever our therapeutic models, listening and questioning in and of themselves are not quite good enough, and that special "knowledges" are helpful as long as we hold them tentatively. For if we do not learn "about" our own cultural selves and the culture of the other, it will be difficult to move beyond our own cultural lenses and biases when we encounter practices that we do not understand or find distasteful; we will not be able to ask the questions that help surface subtle ethnic, gender, or sexuality meanings; and we may not see or hear such meanings when they are right there in front of us. Our own cultural narratives help us to organize our thinking and anchor our lives, but they can also blind us to the unfamiliar and unrecognizable and they can foster injustice. One needs only to think about the gender blindness that dominated the mental health professions for nearly a century to understand how invisible crucial influences on people's lives can be. Moreover, such blindness largely continues today in relation to lesbian, gay, bisexual, and transsexual people. Learning about culture(s) can teach us how to ask good questions in a way that not only helps to surface for our inspection our clients' cultural meanings, but makes it possible for them to hear their own cultural stories in a newly reflective way. It is this cultural questioning process, not cultural characteristics, that has transferability across cultural categories.

On the other hand, we also need to move beyond the curiously static and decontextualized ways in which ethnicity is often theorized, taught, and applied in clinical practice. We have leaned on theories and definitions of ethnicity that stress clusters of attributes and experiences–what might be called "first-order learning"–rather than learning how to learn about culture. We are urged to help people preserve their culture, as if culture were a set of essential and unchanging characteristics, an "it" that is identifiable and preservable in unaltered form. Making the argument in relation to gender, Goldner (1991) argues that an internally consistent idea of gender identity is not possible or even desirable. In her view gender coherence, consistency, conformity, and identity are culturally-mandated normative ideas that become absorbed uncritically and sometimes problematically. I suggest that the same may be said of ethnicity, race, social class, sexuality, and other cultural identities. These normative ideas, in which we are all embedded, encourage stereotyping, narrow our field of possibilities, and prevent us from recognizing the dynamic complexity and continuously changing nature of ethnic, racial, gender, social class, or sexual identity and experience. We are constrained by our nouns, as words like "nature," "identity," and "culture" itself imply these are "things" we can hold for a moment in time. We also find it enormously difficult to either pivot or to shift the center, to divest ourselves of our canons or at least hold them more tentatively, to move our positions, and both to begin with and to enter the experiences and meanings of our informants. The challenge, as bell hooks (1984) frames it, is to move the subjugated experience from margin to center.

My own stance might be described as one of "informed not-knowing" (Shapiro, 1995). "Not-knowing" is used here in the sense that Anderson and Goolishian (1992) use it, to mean that we are never "expert," "right," or in full possession of "the truth." On the other hand, I believe that only if we become as informed as possible–about ourselves and those whom we perceive as different–will we be able to listen in a way that has the potential for surfacing our own cultural biases and recognizing the cultural narratives of the other. Learning "about" culture" from one friend, one book, one client, one trip, gives us the possibility of hearing and seeing even more at the next opportunity; it enriches our repertoire of good and important questions. Furthermore, as investigators, ethnographers, therapists, we are "positioned subjects who are prepared to know certain things and not others" (Rosaldo, 1989, p. 8).

MORE DYNAMIC NOTIONS OF CULTURE: SOME SUGGESTIONS

In this section, I suggest a number of ideas or concepts that have the potential for helping us move away from more essentialist and fixed notions of culture. The terms I use all argue for the "moveable feast" metaphor–that is, the idea that gender, race, and other cultural notions are constantly in motion, changing in meanings and definitions on the parts of both the beholder and the beheld.

Culture Is Performative and Improvisational

Culture is performed; its forms and meanings are situated and communicated in various "contexts for action, interpretation, and evaluation" (Bauman, 1986). We "perform" our cultural stories of gender, ethnicity, race, and so on, as we move through the days in time and space. Furthermore, each performance, each enacted storying, is both unique and at the same time located in and related to the larger social discourses of meaning from which we gather narrative threads, symbols, and ritual possibilities–a combination of tradition and imagination (Laird, 1989). This process can be thought of as "improvisational," a term that I first heard used in reference to "culture" by Myerhoff (1978). She suggested that we make culture up and we make ourselves up as we go along, forcing our experiences to fit into particular sets of meanings. Myerhoff discovered that a group of aging Jews in Venice, California, who thought they were preserving Yiddishkeit, were largely making it and themselves up through highly improvisational story and ritual; these 80- and 90-year-olds, not so much recreating the old as creating the new. Drawing on the work of Kenneth Burke, she suggested they were "dancing an attitude." This is what we do: We dance attitudes.

Culture Is Fluid/Emergent

Culture is contextual. Thus, because no two contexts are ever quite the same, it is always more or less changing and it is always emerging. Who we are changes from moment to moment in shifting settings. We are all multiple cultural selves. I am culturally different when I am in a classroom on the campus of Smith College; vacationing in my Maine cabin in the woods; marching in the Gay, Lesbian, Bisexual March in Washington; driving in heavy traffic by myself; driving in heavy traffic with a casual friend or acquaintance; eating dinner at the college president's house; or visiting my mother in central Florida. What I am aware of is that I change various cultural markers and symbols, as well as my relationships with various stereotyped notions of culture; I alter my language and my topics of conversation, my costuming, my positioning, how much and what I eat or drink. I become more or less feminine or masculine, more or less gay or straight, more or less middle-class, more or less my mother (Protestant, English, and German in heritage) or my father (Catholic, Irish, and French-Canadian). I never wear jeans to the college president's house, I never call anyone an "ass___" when I am performing professionally in public, and I try not to swear in front of my tiny granddaughter. I don't talk about my career in the same way when I am with my family as when I am with my friends or colleagues. I never wear a pink triangle in Maine–one neighbor is a very conservative, rigid, militaristic sort of person (and so I make up ideas about *his* culture!) The point is, that I, like all of us, can dance an attitude.

This is not to trivialize, for example, the importance and centrality to our lives of race, gender, or other aspects of cultural identity. African American family therapist Ken Hardy (1996) has pointed out that race is always salient for him as a person and as a therapist, whether he is working with a White family or another Black man, in a way that it may not (but would, if we could shift the center) feel salient for a White therapist working with a White family. For Hardy, it is always part of the "discourse in the mirrored room" (Hare-Mustin, 1994). Goldner (1988) argued that gender is a fundamental organizing force in family life, even more universal than other mediating variables, such as race, class, or ethnicity. Any cultural categorization or identity–gender, race, class, sexuality–seems more salient at the margins, where there is heightened awareness of how one may be defined as "other" and deprivileged. Furthermore, if one lives on the margins rather than in the center, it is more important to maintain what some have called a "dual perspective"–one informed eye on the dominant culture and the other on one's own. Nevertheless, other than skin color (which itself has different meanings in differing contexts) and one's anatomically distinct characteristics (which can be altered), very little about gender, race, or any other cultural category can be construed as unchanging.

Chicano anthropologist Renato Rosaldo (1989) calls these shifts in context "cultural borderlands," and suggests that they should be regarded as "sites of creative cultural production" (p. 208). Culture is creative and unpredictable, and because it is creative,

> it has its distinctive tempo, and it permits people to develop timing, coordination, and a knack for responding to contingencies. These quali-

ties constitute social grace, which in turn enables an attentive person to be effective in the interpersonal politics of everyday life. (p. 112)

As one of Weston's (1996) informants told her in a comment sure to confuse those who think "lesbian" implies "masculine," or who think that "butch" and "femme" are constant categories that imply imitating heterosexual norms for masculinity and femininity,

> I think I was much more butch before I ever came out. Coming out has been a process of getting in touch with the feminine in me. It gave me the courage to do it and it gave me support to do it by giving me a community that allegedly respects women. When I'm femme, I'm really femme, and when I'm butch, I'm pretty butch. I'd say I'm more butch and femme than most. (p. 111)

Culture Is Intersection

One is never simply a Chicano or a man or gay or working-class or an American. The same person may be, in any one moment, all of these things and much more. None of these categorizations is stable or fixed and no one is ever one of these stories without at the same time all of the others, although one story, one self, may be more salient in one context and time than in another. For a lesbian with children, being woman/mother may be far more important at particular times in her life than her sexual orientation, shaping her activities, her friends, and her presentation of self (Lewin, 1993). As in the turning of a kaleidoscope, variously colored and shaped pieces fall into patterned arrangements where one or the other color or pattern seems to stand out. Recent scholars (e.g., Anderson & Collins, 1992 ; Spelman, 1988) have reminded us that neither race, class, nor gender (and, I would add, any cultural categorization) ever stands alone. Carrying the cultural narrative of a middle-aged, heterosexual, Irish, working-class woman from Boston implies different meanings and different experiences than being a middle-aged heterosexual Irish-American, middle-class woman from Boston; being an Irish working-class woman may have very different meanings than being an American Indian working class woman; and so on. A New York City Puerto Rican man with a doctorate in engineering may speak a constellation of languages: the English of the engineer, of the consultant, of the educated man in his office in the city; another type of English when he is at home with his equally well-educated, White, British American wife; and Puerto Rican Spanish when he returns to rural Puerto Rico for a family reunion. An African American college teacher may use one type of language in her classroom, another in her church, and a third when she returns to her old neighborhood. She is differently African American in each context, drawing on various parts of her ethnic self-story. All are emergently ethnic, differentially performing their ethnicities, drawing on traditional ideas as well as assimilating and acculturating according to the situation. Gender is raced and classed, and shifts in meaning with age, sexual orientation, and other "selves." Similarly, ethnicity is gendered, raced, classed, and so on.

Furthermore, there is tremendous within-group diversity. One can never assume common sets of meanings within any one grouping–not even all middle-class, middle-aged, White, English-descent, heterosexual, feminist, East Coast men share common meanings about gender (or, for that matter, anything else). But the commonalities we've learned about in their life narratives can help us to ask good questions. How is *this* person performing culture?

Culture Is Definitional and Constitutive

Culture is not measurable or generalizable; it cannot be defined, except perhaps in a way that is satisfying to sociologists who are comforted by statistical portraits (which do indeed stimulate certain kinds of important questions)–by the numbers of in-group members who are bar mitzvahed, who intermarry, who attend Sunday school, who march on St. Patrick's Day, or who can speak the native language. Ethnicity, for example, or race cannot be decontextualized and held up for examination and definition, because it is not a thing, an object; it is a narrativized cluster of meanings drawn from past, present, and future that is itself definitional and constitutive. Part of one's cultural identity may be strengthened in situations of contrast or difference– as Bateson implied, these situations provide information. One may feel more "manly" when performing a task that requires physical strength. A woman may develop a heightened consciousness of her usually dormant Jewish heritage–usually dormant–when she is with her British-American in-laws for a holiday. These moments, these points of intersection, lead us (at least in this context) to strengthen certain parts of our cultural selves. Ethnic, gender, social class, and other narratives not only mirror or recreate existing meanings, but create new ones as they are being performed and improvised. The larger culture, the ethnic group, the family, offer us symbols, stereotypes, narratives from which to choose as we, in *bricolage* fashion, constitute and re-constitute ourselves. The adult lesbian or gay "coming-out" experience offers a clear example of how this process can work.

In a fascinating description of the relationships between race, ethnicity, class, and particularly gender on the one hand and sexual orientation on the other, Weston (1996), through extended narrative interviews, pivots around and deconstructs the "tomboy" story as new lesbians draw upon this larger cultural story in a retrospective effort to make sense of current action and to construct a lesbian identity. She says:

> You might think that lesbians would want to dismiss the tomboy-grows-into-a-dyke narrative for the stereotype it is. But drawing upon the inversion model, a woman can use gender to argue for the "realness" of her gay identity. How? She slips continuity into her descriptions of the ways she has gendered herself over the years. She reminds you that her first words were, "Play ball," but forgets to tell you about the time she tried out for cheerleading or homecoming queen. (p. 44)

"Is gendering," Weston asks, "usually consistent over a lifetime, or is consistency an impression produced by the stories people tell about those formative years?" (p. 45). The tomboy narrative, she argues, is raced and classed–a story told far more by white working class women to make sense of their emerging lesbian identities.

Culture Is Political

We know that all stories, whether they are about race, gender, or physical ability, are not equal; that is, people do not have equal voice in shaping their personal narratives, nor do all people have equal opportunities to have their particular stories prevail. Feminist family therapists have demonstrated, for example, how powerfully gendered social discourses and personal gender premises influence how we construct our narratives (Goldner, Penn, Sheinberg, & Walker, 1990; Hare-Mustin, 1994; Laird, 1989). Our personal and family narratives are shaped and constrained by larger cultural narratives that provide the possibilities from which we can choose to make meaning. When these narratives are "problem-saturated" (White & Epston, 1990), invisible, and/or unjust, or simply narrow and constraining, they can, most benignly, inhibit the ways individuals can make sense of themselves and their experiences. More lethally, they can influence the development of shameful, defeating, and even deadly self-narratives.

In sum, I suggest that culture (whether we are talking about gender, age, race, or other cultural categories) is an individual and social construction, a constantly evolving and changing set of meanings that can be understood only in the context of a narrativized past, a cointerpreted present, and a wished-for-future. It is always contextual, emergent, improvisational, transformational, and political; above all, a matter of linguistics or of languaging, of discourse. It is meaning-defined and itself definitional and constitutive.

IMPLICATIONS FOR PRACTICE

Growing out of the above thoughts on culture, and drawing on narrative, constructionist, and other postmodern ideas as they are emerging in the family therapy field, the following suggestions seem relevant to a stance for therapy that is culturally sensitive.

Making "Culture" the Central Metaphor for Therapy

The concept of "culture"—with a small "c" and meant to include any of the sociocultural categorizations we, in interaction with others, make up about ourselves or others make up about us—should be the central metaphor for practice, not a peripheral one. Culture and all of its ingredients are more experience-near, closer to the ground of everyday life and everyday experience, than the more abstract and objectifying metaphors usually invented to label consumers of mental health services.

Culture is constituted through language, through narrative, story, and social discourse. These narratives are performed in private, when the one of our multiple selves is talking to another, or in public, when we are talking to the "other." Culture is put into action by people themselves to constitute and define themselves. The cultural metaphor avoids the machine-like, corporate, experience-distant metaphors of structural and family systems theories, as well as the pathologizing metaphors of psychoanalytic and psychodynamic theories. There is no enmeshed or disengaged dysfunctional family here; nor is there some imagined, tripartite humunculus constructing the rules of the road, directing traffic, and punishing road offenses. Neither is the cultural metaphor as reductionistic as some of the behavioral therapy metaphors, for there is room here for behavior, internal narrative, thought, emotion, language, fantasy, myth, speech, action, and intersubjectivity. It is indeed, a metaphor that allows for movement between inner experience and the outer world.

This does not mean that it is a metaphor without risk. Cultural categorizations may be abused in the service of stereotyping, power politics, and such severe forms of oppression as the appalling practice of "ethnic cleansing" (otherwise known as genocide), violence against women, or gay-bashing. Although "culture" may be misused by some to justify oppression within families or in the larger world—to heighten and exploit "difference," rather than to foster the appreciation of diversity—when used intelligently and empathically, it is a way of entering the lives of people by listening to their own voices, their own everyday experiences.

Taking an Ethnographic Stance

Borrowing from the anthropologist and congruent with the notion of culture as metaphor, several writers in the family field, myself included, have argued for assuming the ethnographic metaphor in practice (Anderson & Goolishian, 1992; Falicov, 1995; Laird, 1989, 1994, 1995, 1996). What this stance most fundamentally is about is figuring out how, when entering the experience of another individual or group of individuals, to be as unfettered as possible with one's own cultural luggage—how to leave at home one's powerful cultural assumptions and to create the conversational spaces wherein the voices of the "other" can emerge. Anderson and Goolishian (1992), in their effort to deconstruct the ethnographic stance, have argued that it is the client who is the expert; as therapists, we do (or should) enter the experience of the other as "not-knowing." Dyche and Zayas (1995) suggest that "cultural naiveté" and "respectful curiosity" are as important as knowledge and skill. Knowledge, or what they call "cultural literacy," they believe, can obscure our views and privilege our own representations over those of our clients.

It is important to point out that we can never completely leave our own cultural assumptions behind. Even the choices we make about to whom to talk or where to position the video camera reflect our own cultural visions and thus direct our gaze. We cannot escape culture; we can only try to meet it on its own terms. This is why it is so vital, as so many scholars have cautioned, to keep working on understanding our own "local knowledges," our own cultural narratives, and to make them as accessible as possible to ourselves and transparent to others.

Furthermore, as I said earlier, we must be highly informed "not-knowers" if we are to ask good questions. What we learn about the culture of one society is not replicable and transferable to another society, just as what we learn about the experiences of one individual or family is not replicable and transferable to another. What *are* replicable and transferable, however, are ideas. Ideas that emerge from one ethnographic or practice experience generate questions to ask of another group, another person. We do not know, in any prior way, the experiences of our informants; leaning on pre-understandings or our own professional "knowledges" may well close us off from understanding the meanings of the person or family in view, creating what it is we expected to see. But as "informed not-knowers," we may bring a wealth of expertise in asking good questions–questions that help to make more visible (both to us and to the "other") their meanings, as well as the sources of those meanings.

Assuming a Narrative Stance

In the last several years, a number of therapists have pioneered and articulated a narrative stance for therapy (e.g., Andersen, 1987; Anderson & Goolishian, 1992; Hoffman, 1992; White & Epston, 1990). The literature on narrative therapy is rapidly expanding, as therapists draw on the work of the pioneers, add to and deepen the ideas, and make applications to various kinds of problems and populations. There is not sufficient space here to review this work. I simply state that I believe the therapeutic stance implied–a stance that is highly respectful, collaborative, and non-hierarchical–is one that encourages the expression of multiple ideas and possibilities; avoids blame or pathologizing; searches for strengths rather than defects; is grounded in a value stance; and fosters transparency on the part of the therapist (i.e., a situating of the therapist's ideas in her or his own experience). It is a stance uniquely suited to culturally sensitive practice.

Deconstructing Cultural Self-Narratives

Although the idea of deconstructing cultural self-narratives is a simple one, it gets lost in translation in many therapies. Many therapists who hope and plan to practice in a culturally sensitive way fail to see or hear the cultural, because their own prior texts are so powerful. Most therapies emphasize "listening." But listening usually means listening for something in particular–for example, for therapist-client relational or transferential material; for evidence to make a diagnosis; for material to confirm our impressions of dysfunction or pathology. Deconstructing the cultural self-narrative also means listening and questioning, but not based on prior assumptions. It means to explore how client cultural meanings and cultural premises (whether linked to race, ethnicity, social class, gender, sexuality, work, religion or mourning, etc.) are being performed, and how they are influencing both the self-story and the problem (Akamatsu, 1995). Furthermore, it means listening "radically," in a way that Weingarten (1995) defines as "authenticating"–a way that is respectful, accepting, and welcoming; a way that searches for the unsaid as well as the said, the invisible as well as the visible.

It is important to recognize that there will be many differing cultural narratives in the same family (those stories also gendered, raced, classed, aged, etc.), responsive to differences in degrees of acculturation, access to new cultural narratives, generational differences, and many other influences. East Indian parents now raising their children in the United States may be hurt and bewildered when their daughter chooses to live in a coed dorm at her university or dates a European American man, while a Chinese American husband may be in despair at the freedoms his wife is claiming in this country. Can we listen in ways that are authenticating and socially just and responsible for all concerned?

Locating Cultural Narrative in the Larger Social Discourse

"Local knowledges" (Geertz, 1983) do not spring simply from the local experience, no matter how intersubjective they may be. For example, in mainstream U.S. society, a teenage girl's profound contempt for her mother is very likely to be connected to a much more pervasive profound contempt of women. For the young girl to accept, value, and identify with her mother may mean envisioning for herself a future filled with both subtle and overt forms of oppression–a future she sees as intolerable. By repudiating her mother, perhaps she can venture down another path in her own adult life. An African American man's depression or his fury toward his wife may have its roots in larger devaluing and invalidating narratives of the Black man's experience. Our self-narratives are embedded in larger social discourses, negotiated over time within relations of knowledge and power (Foucault, 1980), which gain acceptance as "truth." These narratives can be subjugating, they can cut us off from a fuller range of possibilities for ourselves and our lives. Thus, as Hare-Mustin (1994) phrases it, it is crucial to bring these larger social discourses into the mirrored room and to challenge them. Whose stories have prevailed in the shaping of our clients' cultural narratives? Do these stories fit their lived experiences? Are they nurturing, strengthening, and potentiating stories, or are they self-defeating ones? Do they trivialize or even render invisible some of the clients' experiences? Do their self-stories demean their own worth and ideas, and privilege the ideas and interpretations of others? Do their stories contain contradictions or double binds that are invalidating? For example, is a woman of color receiving competing messages about who she is and what she should be choosing from the dominant society and from her own ethnic group? Is a poor woman on Aid to Families with Dependent Children being told on the one hand that she lacks a work ethic, and on the other hand, when she locates work, blamed for neglecting her children because there is no affordable day care? Is a father told on the one hand that it is his job to shoulder the breadwinning responsibilities by working harder or accepting a second job, and on the other faulted for not being available for or nurturing to his children? Is he taught to bury his emotions, to be a warrior, to solve problems and handle challenges aggressively, but punished when he uses these same self-narratives to "discipline" his wife and children? Can transsexuals find any stories that affirm their identity narratives, in which to locate their own isolating and invisible experiences? Are our stories liberating or subjugating?

Resisting Culture or Interrogating the Subjugating Narrative

Most of us have been taught to respect rather than to question differing cultural practices–sometimes even when they seem brutal, such as bride-burning in India, supercision of young males in New Guinea puberty rites, or the clitoridectomy of young females in some African tribes. Taken to its isolationist extreme, a hands-off stance in the face of genocide (e.g., the slaughter of Jews, Cambodians, and Bosnian Muslims) has been tolerated worldwide.

Less dramatically, in our training programs, in our classrooms, and in our therapy offices, we have learned and have taught others to respect differences in what are called ethnic or cultural or class or gender or sexuality values, both within families and in and between ethnic groups. Dilemmas arise, however, when those differences privilege the position of one group or subgroup of a family and deprivilege or subjugate the experiences of another. For example, the Latino gay man (Morales, 1996) or the African American lesbian (Greene, 1994) may be unacceptable in their larger ethnic groups or families, while the voices of the Chinese girl child or even the white, middle class, European American woman may be deprivileged in relation to the family males.

Weingarten (1995) describes, for example, how mothers in this society are constrained by cultural messages about what constitutes "good" and "bad" mothering, so that their effort is to story their lives in ways that will be acceptable within these definitions, not in ways that more accurately reflect their lived experiences. Women's narratives, we have learned, are often silenced, and even their speech genres are ridiculed (Laird, 1989).

Such differences present a dilemma for some narrative therapists, who see bringing culture into the therapy room in a way that challenges dominant discourses as an imposition of personal politics (e.g., Hoffman, 1992). Others, more concerned about subjugation and injustice, take a very different stance. White (1994), for example, argues that every therapeutic act is a political one, and that clients need to be helped to deconstruct not only their self-narratives but also the dominant cultural narratives and discursive practices that constitute their lives. "Deconstruction" means to explore how these dominating discourses are shaped, whose interests they serve and whose they may subjugate, and to expose the marginalized possibilities. How have these dominant and subjugated narratives influenced the "local" story or the story at hand in the clinical situation? This does not mean that therapists deliver their political views as truths, but that they remain sensitive to the spoken stories as well as to the underlying ones that have not been voiced due to lack of power or knowledge. Alertness to the privileging of some narratives in unjust and colonizing dominant discourses allows us to open up conversational spaces in which new and more potentiating narratives may emerge.

Moving Beyond the Mirrored Room Toward a Culturally Just Practice

Finally, and most neglected, is the role of the family therapist in moving beyond the therapeutic conversation to a position between client and community. Minuchin (1991) wonders whether postmodern theory is rescuing us from having to face the evils and hopelessness in the world around us, reducing our concerns to the individual story, when the plots of these stories are often dictated by powerful forces outside the interviewing room.

Justice is raced, gendered, and classed–a lesson cast into bold relief in the last years with the Rodney King beating, the Anita Hill and Clarence Thomas case (Morrison, 1992), the U.S. Navy Tailhook incident, and the ongoing O.J. Simpson saga. It is our responsibility not only to surface cultural stories of oppression and marginalization in people's lives in our offices, but to go beyond the case to help our clients tell their stories in new and larger contexts and to bear witness to those suppressed stories ourselves in the schools, courts, legislatures, and mass media. In other words, we need to add our own voices when those larger cultural discourses do not fairly represent the experiences of our clients and do not allow their stories to be heard.

REFERENCES

Akamatsu, N. N. (1995). The defiant daughter and compliant mother: Multicultural dialogues on woman's role. *In Session: Psychotherapy in Practice, 1*(4), 43-55.

Andersen, T. (1991). *The reflecting team: Dialogues and dialogues about the dialogues.* New York: Norton.

Anderson, H., & Goolishian, H. (1992). The client is the expert: A not-knowing approach to therapy. In S. McNamee & K. Gergen (Eds.), *Therapy as social construction* (pp. 25-39). Newbury Park, CA: Sage Publications.

Anderson, M. L., & Collins, P. H. (Eds.). (1992). *Race, class, and gender: An anthology.* Belmont, CA: Wadsworth Publishing Co.

Bateson, G. (1979). *Mind and nature: A necessary unity.* New York: Dutton.

Bauman, R. (1986). *Story, performance, and event: Contextual studies of oral narrative.* Cambridge: Cambridge University Press.

Dyche, L., & Zayas, L. H. (1995). The value of curiosity and naivete for the cross-cultural therapist. *Family Process 34*(4), 389-399.

Falicov, C. J. (1995). Training to think culturally: A multidimensional framework. *Family Process 34,* 373-388.

Foucault, M. (1980). *Power/knowledge: Selected interviews and other writings.* New York: Pantheon Press.

Friedman, E. (1980). Systems and ceremonies. In E. A. Carter & M. McGoldrick (Eds.), *The family life cycle: A framework for family therapy* (pp. 429-460). New York: Gardner Press.

Geertz, C. (1983). *Local knowledge: Further essays in interpretive anthropology.* New York: Basic Books.

Goldner, V. (1988). Generation and gender: Normative and covert hierarchies. *Family Process 27,* 17-31.

Goldner, V. (1991). Toward a critical relational theory of gender. *Psychoanalytic Dialogues, 1*(3), 249-272.

Goldner, V., Penn, P., Sheinberg, M., & Walker, G. (1990). Gender paradoxes in volatile attachments. *Family Process 29*(4), 343-364.

Greene, B. (1994). Lesbian women of color: Triple jeopardy. In L. Comas-Diaz & B. Greene (Eds.), *Women of color: Integrating ethnic and gender identities in psychotherapy* (pp. 389-427). New York: Guilford Press.

Hardy, K. (1996, June). *The ethics of participation: Bringing culture into the room: A narrative therapy approach. (Reflections).* Paper presented at the annual meeting of the American Family Therapy Academy.

Hare-Mustin, R. (1994). Discourses in the mirrored room: A postmodern analysis of therapy. *Family Process 33*(1), 19-35.

Hoffman, L. (1992), A reflexive stance for family therapy. In S. McNamee and K. J. Gergen (Eds.), *Therapy as social construction* (pp. 2-24). Newbury Park, CA: Sage.

hooks, b. (1984). *Feminist theory from margin to center.* Boston: South End Press.

Laird, J. (1989). Women and stories: Restorying women's self-constructions. In M. McGoldrick, C. Anderson, & F. Walsh (Eds.), *Women in families: A framework for therapy* (pp. 427-450). New York: Norton.

Laird, J. (1994). "Thick description" revisited: Family therapist as anthropologist-constructivist. In E. Sherman & W. J. Reid (Eds*.), Qualitative research in social work* (pp. 175-189). New York: Columbia University Press.

Laird, J. (1995). Family-centered practice in the postmodern era. *Families in Society: The Journal of Contemporary Human Services, 76*(3), 150-162.

Laird, J. (1996). Family-centered practice with lesbian and gay families. *Families in Society: The Journal of Contemporary Human Services, 77*(9), 559-572.

Lewin, E. (1993). *Lesbian mothers. Accounts of gender in American culture.* Ithaca, NY: Cornell University Press.

McGoldrick, M. (1994). Ethnicity, cultural diversity, and normality. In F. Walsh (Ed.), *Normal family processes* (2nd ed., pp. 331-360). New York: Guilford Press.

Minuchin, S. (1991). The seductions of constructivism. *Family Therapy Networker, 15*(5), 47-50.

Montalvo, B. & Gutierrez, M. (1983). A perspective for the use of the cultural dimension in family therapy (pp. 15-32). In C. Falicov (Ed.), *Cultural perspectives in family therapy.* Rockville, MD: Aspen Systems.

Morales, E. (1996). Gender roles among Latino gay and bisexual men: Implications for family and couple relationships. In J. Laird & R.J. Green (Eds.), *Lesbians and gays in couples and families: A handbook for therapists* (pp. 272-297). San Francisco: Jossey-Bass.

Morrison, T. (1992). *Race-ing justice, en-gendering power: Essays on Anita Hill, Clarence Thomas, and the construction of social reality.* New York: Pantheon.

Myerhoff, B. (1978). *Number our days.* New York: Simon and Schuster.

Rosaldo, R. (1989*). Culture & truth: The remaking of social analysis.* Boston: Beacon Press.

Shapiro, V. (1996). Subjugated knowledge and the working alliance: The narratives of Russian Jewish immigrants. *In Session: Psychotherapy in Practice, 1*(4), 9-22.

Spelman, E. (1988). *Inessential woman: Problems of exclusion in feminist thought.* Boston: Beacon Press.

Weingarten, K. (1995). Radical listening: Challenging cultural beliefs for and about mothers. *Journal of Feminist Family Therapy, 7*(1/2), 7-22.

Weston, K. (1996). *Render me, gender me: Lesbians talk sex, class, color, nation, studmuffins . . .* New York: Columbia University Press.

White, M. (1994). *The politics of therapy: Putting to rest the illusion of neutrality.* (Mimeograph). Adelaide, South Australia: Dulwich Family Centre.

White, M., & Epston, D. (1990). *Narrative means to therapeutic ends.* New York: Norton.

Ritual as Therapy, Therapy as Ritual

Judith Davis

SUMMARY. This article comments on the relationship between ritual and therapy with an exploration of two rituals, one from public life and one from clinical practice. Part one focuses on the bar/bat mitzvah ritual (coming-of-age ceremony for 13 year old Jewish adolescents) as a naturally occurring "therapeutic opportunity," and part two, on the way several leading therapists have used variations on the theme of ritual ceremony to create their unique formats for therapy. In particular, Michael White's use of Barbara Myerhoff's (1986) idea of "definitional ceremony," and Lynn Hoffman's use of Tom Andersen's (1987) "reflecting team" idea are highlighted. An illustrative case story is presented and the article ends with a review of parallels between ritual and therapy. *[Article copies available for a fee from The Haworth Document Delivery Service: 1-800-342-9678. E-mail address: <getinfo@haworthpressinc.com> Website: <http://www.haworthpressinc.com>]*

KEYWORDS. Communal practices, bar/bat mitzvah, ritual, therapy, ceremony, reflecting team

RITUAL AS THERAPY

In ritual drama, we show ourselves to ourselves . . .
not only as we are, but as we might yet become.

–Barbara Myerhoff (1986)

Judith Davis, EdD, is a Family Therapist practicing and consulting at Counseling and Assessment Services, University of Massachusetts, Amherst.

Address correspondence to: Judith Davis, 305 Berkshire House, University of Massachusetts, Amherst, MA 01003 (E-mail: judavis@acad.umass.edu).

Deep appreciation is expressed to Lynn Hoffman not only for her generous editing of earlier drafts of this paper, but for her ongoing support and encouragement.

[Haworth co-indexing entry note]: "Ritual as Therapy, Therapy as Ritual." Davis, Judith. Co-published simultaneously in *Journal of Feminist Family Therapy* (The Haworth Press, Inc.) Vol. 11, No. 4, 2000, pp. 115-130; and: *Feminism, Community, and Communication* (ed: Mary E. Olson) The Haworth Press, Inc., 2000, pp. 115-130. Single or multiple copies of this article are available for a fee from The Haworth Document Delivery Service [1-800-342-9678, 9:00 a.m. - 5:00 p.m. (EST). E-mail address: getinfo@haworthpressinc.com].

In 1980, I developed an interest in ritual that I can't shake. During that year, two things happened. First, there was the surprisingly transformative experience of my eldest son's bar mitzvah[1]–transforming not only of him, but more so of me and my marriage. To put it simply, the process of preparing for and participating in our child's rite of passage allowed my husband and me to "grow up" in ways that were totally unanticipated and profoundly liberating–and which led, of course, to many more changes throughout the family (Davis, 1989).

The second thing–a few months later–was the beginning of my training as a family therapist. At that time, the field was experimenting with what were then cutting edge ideas about therapeutic ritual. Pioneered by the Milan team (Palazzoli, 1977), these were paradoxical prescriptions for enactments that were meant to interrupt the "dysfunctional patterns" keeping the family "stuck" and unable to move along on the proverbial life cycle. As I sat struggling through the delivery of one of the elaborate rituals devised by my supervisor[2] and colleagues behind the mirror, I began to wonder what therapists could learn from naturally occurring cultural or religious life cycle rituals. Was what I experienced idiosyncratic to my family's particular story or was there an actual connection between ritual and health?

This question became the basis of my dissertation research, several professional pieces (Davis, 1988, 1990,1995), and ultimately a book for parents preparing for their child's bar/bat mitzvah (Davis, 1998). You would think that by now I'd have had enough of this topic, but in fact, it continues to intrigue me. As the field of family therapy focuses increasingly on concepts like restorying (White, 1997), performative psychology (Holtzman and Newman, 1996), and communal practices (Hoffman, 1999), the bar/bat mitzvah stands as an example of family-community interaction that could well be instructive. As sociologist Phillip Slater (1974) says,

> In a simple community when a family crisis occurs, people run into the street and the community gathers to mediate, nourish and absorb. As a community becomes larger and less integrated, the capacity of the family to generate drama does not change, but it can no longer be shared. The community becomes privatized, the family isolated, the streets empty . . . referral agencies, mental hospitals, prisons and nursing homes are a few of the tardy, impersonal, inhumane, and generally rather dilapidated mechanisms we have evolved to replace this naïve responsivity.

To the extent that the bar/bat mitzvah ceremony in the synagogue is the public marker of the family's transition from a family with a child, to a family with a teenager, the family's developmental "crisis" is brought–if not into the street–onto the *bimah* [stage] where the community/congregation can witness, nourish and celebrate the good changes. Given that many therapists relegate such an event to the realm of religion and then explore it no further, I offer here some ideas about the bar/bat mitzvah experience as a paradigmatic example of how public life cycle ceremonies enable our evolving sense of a good self precisely to the degree that they engage a community of loving witnesses. (The parallels for other life cycle ceremonies and for other religions/cultures can be easily drawn, but are beyond the scope of this paper.)

The Ritual of Bar/Bat Mitzvah

The complexity and power of the contemporary American bar/bat mitzvah are sorely underestimated. The event is not simply what it looks like-a religious ceremony and a big (sometimes very big) birthday party. Neither is it simply the child's "coming of age" in the Jewish community (forever after counted among the adults). Instead, it is, to varying degrees and with varying levels of consciousness, a major transitional moment for the entire three generational family-a milestone with ripples reverberating throughout the extended system.

For the child, the ritual ordeal is prescribed and public. It is a "trial by recitation" (Arlow, 1951), a public demonstration of learning, accomplishment and commitment. After months of intensive study and practice, the child ascends to the center of the ritual space, blesses the Torah for the first time, chants the appropriate prayers and texts, delivers an interpretive speech and then-with a huge sigh of relief-stands basking in the love, pride, congratulations and goodwill streaming from all directions. Mazel tov! What a way to begin one's teens.

For the parents, on the other hand, this trial by ritual is amorphous and private. Behind the scenes, and beginning months, in some cases, years, before the first guest arrives, the parents are responsible for creating the space in which this child can shine. Unlike weddings where everyone expects the preparation period to be stressful, most first time bar/bat mitzvah parents are totally unprepared for the amount of stress they experience and the range of emotions it evokes. Told only that this is "such a '*simcha*' (joyous event)," they are often shocked by all of the mixed feelings they are encountering.

What these families and those who consult with them need to know is that this process of preparing for a child's bar/bat is not only joyous, but inherently stressful as well. In addition to the fact that their child is becoming an adolescent, the parents are also evolving in terms of the changing family life cycle. The bar mitzvah does not simply reflect new realities, it helps create them. Like it or not, still married or not, these parents are having to renegotiate a whole range of relationships and meanings. They are having to deal with their differences, whatever they are, over this child's initiation into Jewish responsibility, not to mention into adolescence. And then there is the issue of their own parents: by now they are aging visibly and if the care-taking reversals have not yet begun, they are looming on the horizon. No wonder bar/bat mitzvah parents feel the weight of this event. They are responding to and shaping change in relation to their child, their parents, their partners and themselves.

And of course there's more. All of their unresolved issues regarding faith, religion, ethnicity that have been dormant since their own youths, are once again active. What does this religious/cultural event for their child bring up for them as children of their parents? What unfinished stories are being re-evoked? These themes are often difficult even when both parents are Jewish, but in today's increasingly intermarried and remarried population, the intra and intergenerational complexities can be staggering. And speaking of complexities, one has only to imagine the permutations when it is a single parent, interracial, gay or lesbian family approaching this moment.

Finally, the event itself. Having chosen to mark their child's thirteenth birthday with a religious ritual that has a long history and many expectations surrounding it, they have taken on the challenge of orchestrating the biggest, costliest, most emotion-filled happening for which they have ever been responsible. Never before have they, as "the adults here," brought together all of the people who are important in their lives and in the life of their child to meet at a single event at once so personal and so public. For the first time they will be encountering with one face all of their relatives, neighbors, colleagues and friends from over the years. It is a huge emotional as well as logistical undertaking. Family therapist and Rabbi Ed Friedman (1981) calls the bar/bat mitzvah weekend "the original encounter marathon."

To the extent that an initiation ritual has to be an ordeal, the bar/bat mitzvah qualifies. It is a trial-in different ways-for all members of the family, and the sense of achievement they each derive at its successful conclusion is enormous, most often far exceeding their expectations.

How the Bar/Bat Mitzvah Works Therapeutically[3]

The bar/bat mitzvah "works" in many different, but complementary ways. Most basically, it works by providing participants with a familiar format, a safe, protected structure for making and marking transitions. It is a powerful vehicle for expressing both grief and joy as children, parents and grandparents move into new life phases. With its rhythmic symbols and ceremony, the ritual guides them almost hypnotically into new territory. It makes their journeys public and positive.

In the context of this highly charged atmosphere, the celebrants and those who have come to be with them draw closer to one another, experiencing a profound sense of connectedness. It is as if the usual boundaries momentarily melt. Anthropologist Victor Turner (1977) calls this an experience of *communitas*. One bat mitzvah mother with whom I spoke described the experience as being "love bombed." Every time she turned and took a peek at the sea of friends and family seated behind her in the synagogue, she felt overwhelmed. "They were smiling at me, nodding at me, winking, crying. It just filled me with love."

The bar/bat mitzvah ritual also has potential for healing in the way it works symbolically not only to mark borders, but to make connections. The bar/bat mitzvah is the child's proclamation of growing maturity and eventual independence, but it is a proclamation being made in the embrace of the family and in the center of its tradition. It is a proclamation of increasing distance, yet paradoxically, also one of connection and continuity. "Yes," the child is saying, "I am growing up and away, but I will always be connected to my family, its culture, and its tradition." In the magical way of all ritual, the bar/bat mitzvah is an act of anchoring that ultimately enables the celebrant's capacity to fly.

Through the bar/bat mitzvah, the child enters the "betwixt and between" years with an expression of both separation and connection that is developmentally perfect. It is perfect because it represents the paradoxical needs for both distance and closeness that emerging adolescents are necessarily negotiating as they evolve their ideas about themselves as young people in relationship to parents and peers. (See Dickerson et al., "Challenging Developmental Truths: Separating from Separation,"1994.) And given that the adolescents' stories and their parents' stories are so interwoven, the bar/bat mitzvah's capacity to help with these shifting stories is developmentally perfect for them as well. Just as the experience helps children develop confidence in themselves, it helps parents have confidence in them, and in their own ability to know how much to hold on and how much to let go–not only as parents, but as partners and as children themselves.

There is yet another way in which the bar/bat mitzvah works to promote growth and transformation. This "work" is much more prosaic, almost accidental, and generally goes unnoticed. It happens during the planning period, the months before the event when the family is immersed in the nitty-gritty decisions about whom to invite, where to house them, what to feed them, where to seat them, what kind of party to have, what kind of music to play, etc. These pragmatic decisions are, of course, about managing the size, shape, and feel of the event, but they are also about much more. Whether their potential is noticed consciously or not, these decisions and the manner in which they are made often turn out to be opportunities for evolving new ways of relating, new ways that the family's new life circumstances demand. Such decisions about everything from prayers to parties, guest lists to thank you notes, are really decisions about relationships. They are the therapeutic opportunities hidden in the ritual's details, the openings that become available during these months that Friedman (1980) calls "hinges of time," times "when the system is most open to change."

Thought of in this way, the preparation details are often opportunities for embodying values parents want to transmit, for enacting the stories by which they want to know themselves. One example, in particular, comes to mind. I call it *"Bubbie's Feet."* One day when consulting to a family preparing for a bar mitzvah, I asked how they had chosen the date–an innocuous query to ease into an interview. The question was met by silence and puzzled looks all around. It was hard to remember a decision made so many months earlier. Then Donnie, the bar mitzvah boy, piped up with a smile: "It's because of Bubbie's feet!" "Bubbie's feet?" I asked. "Yeah, my grandmother lives in Florida and she has bad feet. So we had to make my bar mitzvah in May instead of in February, when my birthday really is, so it wouldn't snow and Bubbie could wear open shoes."

Embedded in this one small, seemingly mundane detail, is a whole world of meaning: the value of honoring the past, the desire to solidify connections between generations, the importance of compassion. Embedded also, it turns out, was a story of healing. For as long as he could remember, Donnie's father, Mark, had been in conflict with his own parents. As a young man, Mark had dramatically rejected their "smothering" old-world demands and had kept himself emotionally as well as physically distant. At some unspoken level, his son's upcoming bar mitzvah was Mark's message to his parents about love and about reconnection. *Zayda,* Donnie's grandfather, had died years ago, so Bubbie just *had* to be there. This message was further enacted during the ceremony when, after Donnie had completed his part, Mark came up to the *bimah* to say some words of praise and appreciation. Barely choking back his tears, Mark presented his son with the ritual objects that had been his father's–his old *tallis* (prayer shawl), *teffilin* (prophylactories) and dog-eared prayer book–and as he put them, one by one, in his son's hands, he spoke to him about what his father used to tell him as a child–that the world was good–and about what he might have said to his grandson had he been alive on this day. It was a powerful moment.

Ritual Responsivity

In an age when most traditional beliefs and ritual practices are being abandoned, why is the bar/bat mitzvah so popular? I believe the reasons go beyond the usual explanations about nostalgia, guilt and marketplace manipulation, and beyond even the broader, more benign sociological and psychological explanations that have been put forth (Davis, 1998; Kosman, 1999; Schoenfeld, 1990). What I believe is that something authentic is happening on that ritual stage and whatever it is–whatever combination of "truths" are in play–it is that authenticity that keeps the practice of bar/bat mitzvah alive.

This use of the word "authentic" has nothing to do with ideas about the "true self." Instead, I am using it to describe the process that happens *between* the performers of a powerful public ritual and those who participate as witnesses when they authenticate the sense of transformation in each other. The drama on the ritual stage (like Slater's family drama in the street) engages the community's "naïve responsivity," its capacity to be moved in coordination with the family's movement. The family in the center of the ritual ceremony enters the public space expecting a response to its call, and those drawn into its experience come expecting to respond. Both the performers and the witnesses engage with each other through a stream of shared experiences and meanings that connect back to the past and into the future. This is an example of what Kenneth Gergen (1998), in his discussion of our socially constructed relations, calls "harmonies of coordination." The performance is *for* the witnesses, those gathered, those remembered, and those anticipated. In the "interplay of words, positions, distances, touchings and more" (Gergen, 1998), the harmonic coordinations that emerge are natural, compelling, and healing. In that liminal, trance-like moment of communitas, something new is being made possible. Something poignantly hopeful is happening, and all who are engaged are changed. Ritual performance," says Myerhoff (1992), "has the capacity to make the impossible momentarily beyond question."

THERAPY AS RITUAL

Ritual is our original form of therapy.

–Ed Friedman (1982)

Michael White (1995, 1997) talks about a similar form of public authenticating. In his discussion of therapy as "definitional ceremony" (Myerhoff, 1986), he talks about those seeking consultation as persons at the center of the ceremony and those who are members of the listening/audience group as "outsider witnesses." These witnesses to the performance, he says, contribute to the "acknowledgement and to the authentication of the person's knowledge claims" about her/himself.

Having listened to the story told by the person in the center of the ceremony, these witnesses then "respond with a retelling of the stories told and of the knowledge and skills experienced" during that telling. During the period in which the outsider witnesses are listening, they are attending not only to what in the story "captures their attention," but in what ways those aspects of the story "trigger images of their own lives" (1997). White goes on to say that

> For outsider-witness group members, the reverberations that are set off by these therapeutic conversations frequently touch on many experiences long forgotten, and as well, endow previously remembered experiences with a new significance . . . This engagement of outsider witness group members is not neutral in regard to its effects on the shape of their own lives-it is constitutive.

Even if the audience-White's witnesses or the bar/bat mitzvah child's relatives-came simply as audience prepared only to applaud[4] the celebrant's production, that production resonates with their own experience and in that resonance they, too, are changed. Myerhoff (1992) puts it this way: "When the performance is successful, the private is made public and the public (performance) becomes integrated into our private identities." Something does change both for the celebrants and for the witnesses.

The parallels between the family on the ritual stage and the family in therapy are apparent and becoming more so as other therapists such as Peggy Penn and Marilyn Frankfurt (1998) also explore the connections between client as performer and therapist as audience. In the following quote, in which they are discussing a case that includes the client's reading his writing aloud, they are talking about the "relational aesthetics" of the therapy session. They could as easily be describing the aesthetics of ritual. They say

> Something new emerges in this witnessed telling to others. When the client . . . becomes drawn creatively, dramatically, into this experience of performance . . . the client's feelings intensify, a relational process takes place between all of us-the family members, therapists and associates as witnesses and the client as central performer. *While the performance* is in progress, we lend ourselves cognitively, imaginatively and viscerally to one another. It's almost mysterious. We all become something more than the sum of the individual ingredients of the experience. (pp. 28-29)

An Alternative Bar Mitzvah

As a more detailed example of therapy as ritual, the following is a story of a similar ceremony. It took place during a period several years ago when I was travelling with Lynn Hoffman to consult with the staff of a child protection agency in Northern Massachusetts, using the reflecting team idea. This format, developed by Norwegian psychiatrist Tom Andersen (1987), has been widely adopted by many clinicians and trainers.[5] Michael White, for instance, used it to put into practice his ideas about definitional ceremonies.

Jack and the Beanstalk

Jack (not his real name) was 12 when we met him. The family's therapist, Jeanne Ingress, had been very concerned about what was going on in the family. Jack had a history of getting into violent fights at school. He had just been suspended because of another fight after which the teacher had found a knife in his pocket. Six months earlier he had been sent to a psychiatric hospital for observation, and we learned later that he was still on medication when we met him. Although he had been doing much better after returning from the hospital, this latest incident put him in great jeopardy. Jack's mother Tammy had told Jeanne that she had been crying all morning, afraid that her son would now be taken away from her. She was eager to come in, despite the fact that our consulting session included over 25 people from two regional sites.

When Jack and his mother arrived, the observers were seated around the edge of the large room. Additional chairs had been arranged in a semi-circle at one end to accommodate Jeanne, a social worker who was seeing the two other children, Jack, Tammy, Lynn and myself. Lynn opened the conversation by introducing everyone and explaining what we would be doing together. She described the reflecting team format and said that we would start by talking with the family's therapist, since it was she who had requested the consultation, and then move to the family. She also explained the use of the camera and received the family's permission to videotape.

As promised, Lynn asked Jeanne her perspective. What Jeanne described was a history of abuse and violence: Not only had Jack been physically abused in the past, but he had watched often as his mother was being beaten by her boyfriend. A couple of years earlier, two older neighborhood girls had molested Jack sexually, and he had been present when the boyfriend of one of these girls slashed his wrist in the family's kitchen.

In this description we began hearing what Lynn calls the "cascade of violence" explanation for troubled males: if a boy is victimized and abused when young and defenseless, the rage he retains will cause him to victimize others when he gets older. Indeed, this idea was held so strongly by everyone in and around the family that Tammy was afraid that Jack would either hurt or kill someone, or get hurt or killed himself. Expectations were very grim. Although this explanation was logical, it was not helpful. As part of a general view of the pathology of poverty, it reinforced what was already a very negative situation.

As consultants, Lynn and I were listening for an alternative story–one that would point to a more hopeful future. We were listening for any information that did not fit with the cascade view. Finally some details emerged that struck a different note. During the time Tammy was living with her violent boyfriend, Jack told the police that the man had sexually molested him. No one ever knew if it was true or not, but Jack later said that he had made up the story to get the boyfriend out of the house. "He's a real protector," Jeanne said, and we agreed.

Another point came out during our inquiry into this latest fight. Jack told us that he had been protecting a friend from a bigger boy who was attacking him, a bully who often picked on Jack's younger brother as well. The jackknife, it turned out, had been in his pocket from a hike he had taken the day before. Here, Jeanne described him as a caretaker, but "one who doesn't know how to control himself." Tammy then expressed her worry that Jack might lash out and really hurt someone. "And then I might lose him," she said, "and don't want to see him lose his family." "And you don't want to lose him," Lynn echoed. "No," replied Tammy, looking into Jack's eyes, "I don't. I've had him since he was inside of me. I don't want to lose this kid."

We then asked the reflecting team to speak. As I joined the clinicians who had earlier volunteered to be on the team, I reminded the family that we wanted the therapists to talk with each other in the presence of the family rather than someplace where they couldn't be heard. "So please excuse our backs," I said, "We don't mean to be rude, we just wanted you and Jack to have the opportunity to listen in and not have to respond." Tammy got the idea immediately. "So we just sit back?" she asked. "Right," I answered, "We're the ones on stage now."

In the course of the reflecting conversation, a very different story about Jack emerged. As the first to speak, I commented on the difference between what I had expected and what I'd experienced. I said that having listened to the therapist's description of the family we were about to meet—one which had endured so much pain, violence and abuse—I found myself expecting to meet a "really angry" adolescent, someone who got into all these fights, someone his mother would have to be dragging into the meeting. Instead, what struck me most as I was listening to them talk, was the love that seemed so evident. Beyond anything they said, it was Jack's love for his mother, and her love for him that seemed to permeate everything. Jack's sweetness and his mother's appreciation of that sweetness was what was most compelling for me.

The next reflecting person was the director of the clinic. He also spoke of surprise. He had expected to meet a family "beaten down" by their experience. Instead, what he saw was a son who was willing to go to great lengths to protect his mother, brother, and friend, and a mother who was clearly willing to go to any ends to get whatever she needed for her son. The third reflector, commenting on what the conversation was bringing up for her, spoke about the idea of justice. She said, "Jack has this great sense of justice and he's ready to get in there and fight and do whatever he needs to do, and unfortunately there have been times when that has gotten him in trouble."

Closing the loop, I spoke to this last speaker about how helpful her idea of justice was for me in thinking about this family's story. "Maybe anger was a part of the story, a chapter," I said, "but not the title of the book. Justice was more like it. Jack was this little 'crusader for justice.' "

Jack and his mother listened intently to this conversation about their conversation. The surprise and pleasure of hearing themselves discussed in this way was evident both on their faces and in the way they kept stealing glances at each other and exchanging smiles.

Following the reflections, Jack told us he had not expected this many people. Although Tammy knew there would be a large group, she hadn't conveyed this to her son. As we commented on how "cool" he had remained despite his surprise, Lynn asked Jack if he'd ever wanted to be an actor. It was an impulsive question, but sure enough, he had! He wished, he said, that he could be the hero on a program called Night Rider (a sort of James Bond program for kids). Lynn volunteered that she was imagining that if he ever did a play, it would be called "Jack the Giant Killer." "Do you know that story?" she asked. He did. In fact, he actually owned the book and treasured it. For her part, Jeanne's response to the reflecting conversation was to think about what it was like for Jack, who had always been told he was "a bad boy," to hear now that he was trying to fight for justice.

As planned, we then went on to a second round of reflections and heard from the larger group. Lynn had earlier instructed them to listen "as if" they were the teachers, DSS workers, school principal, etc. involved with the family. In addition, I suggested they also think about what it might be like if these teachers and other helpers were to be introduced to the family through this idea of justice, and to Jack as a kind of "giant killer" who, when he feels there is an injustice, acts in ways that look like anger. If this were another piece of the story that could be given to them, how might they perceive this family differently? How might their concerns about safety be handled? From this round of reflections, there emerged many more thoughts supporting and amplifying the family's new story, but this time including important ideas around safety.

Towards the end of the session, Lynn, again on impulse, asked the family for a grade. "Jack, what grade would you give this way of working together?" "A-plus," he answered. "Why?" she asked. "Because," Jack answered, "you care a lot."

We then discussed ways of getting this enlarged picture of the family into the record. "Do you mean there is more bad showing than there is good?" Tammy asked, "And if you see good, why doesn't that come out more?" "Come out or just get into the record," I answered. "Well, in my opinion," Tammy explained, "people *see* the wrongs, hear the wrongs, so they're not going to want to know nothing about you. That's the way I see it." "So what about this record?" Lynn asked. Would it be helpful for other people who don't know this aspect of the family to see this video?" "I'd like Greg, my fiancé to see it," Tammy answered. "Yeah, and my brother and sister," Jack added. "And the teachers and the principal," Tammy concluded.

After talking with Tammy and Jeanne about how to make these showings possible, Lynn stood up to begin saying good-bye. But Tammy, pointing to the camera, objected, saying that we had forgotten one thing: The cameraman (Dick Baldwin, one of the clinic's coordinators and its videographer) had been left out. Here Lynn asked Jack if he would like to hold the video while Dick spoke. "You can be the cameraman," Tammy said, encouraging her son.

It was a very dramatic moment. Prior to this exchange, Jack had been sitting hunched over as if zoning out, but now he leapt up alertly and the camera caught his smiling face as he strode toward the camera and exchanged places with Dick. For all who were present, this brief moment seemed magical, almost as if the "new boy" inside the "old boy" had suddenly come out. As anthropologist Edward Bruner (1986) puts it, "It is in the performance that stories become transformative." Mazel tov, Jack!

The interview ended on this very positive note. In the weeks that followed, Jeanne and Tammy were able to get Jack into a smaller, more intimate school where he began to do very well. The other children were also continuing to be seen in therapy. One colleague, very impressed by Jeanne's efforts, said that she had never known a family where the therapist was able to get them so much help.

Although there were still many rough spots over the next few years, the family persevered. Tammy married her new boyfriend, a man who seemed more like the responsible father Jack never had, and Jack himself shot up like a beanstalk (what else?). He took pride in doing well in school and in learning to walk away from fights. On the several occasions when Jeanne brought us in to visit the family, we taped our interviews, and with the family's permission, showed them at conferences abroad. We no longer had a reflecting team, so we brought back witnessing messages from workshop participants instead. On one occasion, Jack actually wrote a letter back to one of the distant witnesses who had written to him about how his story had connected to hers.

The last time we saw Jeanne and the family, we learned that Jack had been sexually approached by the family's rich and locally powerful landlord. He was well known in the neighborhood for molesting children. Courageously, Jack and his mother took him to court. They lost their apartment in the short term, but the landlord ended up on the registry of sex offenders. As witnesses to all of these developments, Lynn and I sent Jeanne and the family a "Certificate of Appreciation," an idea we learned from David Epston and Michael

White (1990). It commented on their many achievements over the four years during which we had been privileged to be consulting with them.

Parallels Between Ritual and Therapy

If ritual is humankind's original form of therapy, the many parallels between them make sense: Both are suspensions: "disruptions of normal dialogue" (White, 1997), "interruptions in the flow of every day life" (Frankfurt and Penn, 1998). Both are public, structured occasions with prescribed formats, actions, and mutually agreed upon roles. In classic ritual, we talk about the tripartite process of "breach, transition, and reincorporation" (van Gennep, 1909). In therapy, we talk about the parallel "telling, retelling, and retelling of the retelling" (White, 1997).

In the "breach," the conversation in which clients tell their story to the therapist stops. In the "transition," the change is twofold. Not only do the listeners become tellers and the tellers, listeners, but in this liminal space of reversals, the retelling of the story transforms the story. The transformative act (of blessing the Torah, of co-authoring a new story) is magical, very hard to describe. Something wondrous is happening, if only for a few seconds, as meanings shift and new perceptions suddenly emerge. The third stage, the "reincorporation," is the retelling of the retelling, the process of integrating the new story into the one the participants came in with. The public becomes the private again.

In addition, both ritual and therapy take place in a sacred space, whether sanctuary or clinic; both make use of sacred words, whether incantations or reflections; and both make use of ritual symbols, whether stained glass windows or one way screens. Both are "forms of communication in which identities are constituted and negotiated" (Olson, 1999), and both are discourses that depend heavily on metaphor, the language that "moves meaning in the mind" (Frankfurt and Penn, 1998).

The experience of ritual and therapy are also cathartic, as Michael White makes clear in his discussion of the definitional ceremony (1997). He explains catharsis not in the old sense of emotional release, but in the sense of moving people to a place they had not been before. He defines it as a powerful experience that replaces the humanist psychologist's idea about becoming "who we really are" with the idea of becoming "other than we were." To say it differently, both ritual and therapy are reflexive social dramas that build intensity as story lines thicken, meanings get made, and participants become increasingly engaged with one another. This is a process of responsivity that Slater, in his discussion of the community in the street, calls naïve, that John Lannaman (1998), in his discussion of the way we make meaning, calls "embodied," and that I, in this exploration of transitional rites, might go so far as to call sacred. It's no wonder that the words holy and health are etymologically linked.

CONCLUSION

In ritual performance, says Myerhoff (1982), doing is believing. We are performing an act of imagination, one that has the possibility of transforming what "is" into "what yet could be." The bar/bat mitzvah is a public enactment for progeny, parents and peers, of the family's most hopeful "knowledges" about itself. Jack's similar performance and Jeanne's inspired relationship with the family were also enactments of hope, witnessed not only by Lynn and myself, but by all those whose authenticating messages we brought with us. In the liminal or "threshold" space of the ritual act, something full of promise is being performed. In the case of Jack's alternative rite of passage, we like to believe, for the moment at least, that a little boy who seemed destined either for a hospital or a jail cell became a giant-killer instead.

ENDNOTES

1. Literally translated, bar mitzvah means "son of the commandments" and bat mitzvah means "daughter of the commandments." The term refers both to the celebrant and to the ceremony. In Jewish tradition, the ceremony marks the child's entrance into (Jewish) adulthood, where, among other things, he or she can now be counted in the quorum required for communal prayer. Grammatically, the child does not "get bar/bat mitzvahed," but "becomes" a Bar or a Bat Mitzvah.
2. It was my great good fortune to be training at that time with Evan Imber Black, an extraordinary teacher and mentor.
3. This section is a modified excerpt from my book, *Whose Bar/Bat Mitzvah Is This, Anyway?*
4. See Michael White's (1997) fascinating exploration of the idea of applause.
5. The reflecting team was different from its precursor, the Milan-style systemic team, in that instead of the professionals sitting behind a screen and consulting with each other privately, they were positioned so that their conversation could be overheard by the family who could then comment on what the professionals had said.

REFERENCES

Andersen, T. (1987) The reflecting team: Dialogue and meta-dialogue in clinical work. *Family Process*: 26: 415-428.

Arlow, J. A. (1951). A psychoanalytic study of a religious initiation rite: Bar mitzvah. In R.S. Eissler, A. Freud, H. Hartmann, and L.Kils (Eds.). *Psychoanalytic study of the child*: Vol. 6 (pp.364-374). New York: International Universities Press.

Bruner, E. (1986). Introduction. In V. Turner and E. Bruner (Eds.). *The anthropology of experience.* Urbana and Chicago: University of Illinois Press.

Davis, J. (1988). Mazel tov: The bar mitzvah as a multigenerational ritual of change and continuity. In E. Imber-Black, J. Roberts, and R. Whiting (Eds.). *Rituals in families and family therapy.* New York: W.W. Norton.

Davis, J. (July, 1989). The bar mitzvah triangle: A family story. *The Family Therapy Networker.*

Davis, J. (1990). Bar mitzvah: A family systems analysis. In S. Fishbane and J. Lighthouse, (Eds.). *Essays in the social scientific study of Judaism and Jewish society.* Montreal: Department of Religion, Concordia University Press.

Davis, J. (1995). The bar mitzvah balabustah: Mother's role in the family's rite of passage. In M. Sacks, (Ed.). *Active voices: Women in Jewish culture.* University of Illinois Press.

Davis, J. (1998). *Whose bar/bat mitzvah is this anyway: A guide for parents through the family's rite of passage.* New York: St. Martin's Press.

Dickerson, V., Zimmerman, J. and Berndt, L. (1994). Challenging Developmental Truths: Separating from separation. *Dulwich Centre Newsletter,* No 4.

Frankfurt, M. and Penn, P. (1998). Client voices and relational aesthetics: A correspondence. *Journal of Systemic Therapies,* Vol. 17, No. 4:27-38.

Friedman, E. H. (1980). Systems and ceremonies: A family view of rites of passage. In E. A. Carter and M. McGoldrick, (Eds.). *The family life cycle* (pp.429-460) New York: Gardner Press.

Friedman, E. H. (1981, Spring). Bar mitzvah when parents are no longer partners. *Journal of Reform Judaism,* 28:53-66.

Friedman, E. H. (1982). Personal communication.

Gergen, K. (1998). The place of materiality in a constructed world. *Family Process,* 37: 415-419.

Hoffman, L. (1999). A communal perspective for postmodern therapies. *Journal of Feminist Family Therapy* (in press).

Kosmin, B. (1999). Coming of age in the conservative synagogue: The b'nai mitzvah class of 5755. Unpublished paper for the *Institute for Jewish Policy Research,* London, England.

Lannamann, J. W. (1998). Social Construction and materiality: The limits of indeterminacy in therapeutic settings. *Family Process,* 37:393-413.

Myerhoff, B. (1982). Life history among the elderly: Performance, visibility, and re-membering. In Jay Ruby (Ed.), *A crack in the mirror: Reflexive perspectives in anthropology.* Philadelphia: University of Pennsylvania Press.

Myerhoff, B. (1986). Life not death in Venice: Its second life. In V. Turner and E.M. Bruner (Eds.), *The anthropology of experience.* Urbana and Chicago: University of Illinois Press.

Myerhoff, B. (1992). *Remembered lives: The work of ritual, storytelling, and growing older.* Ann Arbor: The University of Michigan Press.

Newman, F. and Holtzman, L. (1996). *Unscientific psychology.* Westport CT: Praeger.

Olson, M. (1999). Unpublished correspondence.

Palazzoli, M.S., Boscolo, L., Cecchin, G., and Prata, G. (1977). Family rituals: A powerful tool in family therapy. *Family Process.* 16:445-453.

Schoenfeld, S. (1990). Some aspects of the social significance of the bar/bat mitzvah celebrations. pp. 277-304. In S. Fishbane and J. Lighthouse (Eds.). *Essays in the social scientific study of Judaism and Jewish society.* Montreal: Department of Religion, Concordia University.

Slater, P. (1974). *Earthwalk.* New York: Bantam Books.

White, M. (1997). *Narratives of therapists' lives.* Adelaide, South Australia: Dulwich Center Publications.

Turner, V. (1969). *The ritual process: Structure and anti-structure.* Chicago: Aldine Publishing Co.

Turner, V. (1977). Variations on a theme of liminality. In S. Moore and B. Myerhoff (Eds.), *Secular Ritual.* Assem, Holland: Van Gorcum Press.

van Gennep (1909). *Les rites de passage.* London, England: Routledge Kegan Paul, Translated by M. B. Vizedom and G. L. Caffee and republished 1960. Chicago: University of Chicago Press.

White, M. (1995). *Re-authoring lives: Interviews and essays.* Adelaide, Australia: Dulwich Centre Publications.

White, M. (1997). *Narratives of therapists' lives.* Adelaide, Australia: Dulwich Centre Publications.

White, M. and Epston, D. (1990). *Narrative means to therapeutic ends.* New York/London: W.W. Norton and Co.

Feminism in the Middle East: Reflections on Ethnographic Research in Lebanon

Catherine K. Kikoski

SUMMARY. There is a history of feminism that is rooted in the Middle East. And there is a future. Patriarchy, tradition and religious conservatism in the area have led women to struggle for emancipation and equality on many levels. This ethnographic research study in the Middle East gives voice to a young generation of women who reveal their own unique brand of feminism. The overarching theme of this research seems to be a universal yearning of women to be free to express themselves, and to realize their goals and dreams in their own ways, and in their own cultural contexts. They have a clear vision of themselves in their society, and the role they must play to realize their vision: to lead more autonomous lives, but not at the price of the relationships that sustain and nourish them. In this way, culture punctuates feminism. *[Article copies available for a fee from The Haworth Document Delivery Service: 1-800-342-9678. E-mail address: <getinfo@haworthpressinc.com> Website: <http://www.haworthpressinc.com>]*

KEYWORDS. Lebanon, feminism, ethnography, Middle East

The crisis in feminism ... has given us a wider audience for cross-cultural work on gender and women. Feminist ethnographies that try to

---

Catherine K. Kikoski, EdD, is Professor in the Department of Marriage and Family Therapy, Saint Joseph College, 1678 Asylum Avenue, West Hartford, CT 06117 (E-mail: ckikoski@sjc.edu).

[Haworth co-indexing entry note]: "Feminism in the Middle East: Reflections on Ethnographic Research in Lebanon." Kikoski, Catherine, K. Co-published simultaneously in *Journal of Feminist Family Therapy* (The Haworth Press, Inc.) Vol. 11, No. 4, 2000, pp. 131-146; and: *Feminsm, Community, and Communication* (ed: Mary E. Olson) The Haworth Press, Inc., 2000, pp. 131-146. Single or multiple copies of this article are available for a fee from The Haworth Document Delivery Service [1-800-342-9678, 9:00 a.m. - 5:00 p.m. (EST). E-mail address: getinfo@haworthpressinc.com].

© 2000 by The Haworth Press, Inc. All rights reserved.

bring to life what it means to be a woman in other places and under different conditions, ethnographies that explore what work, marriage, motherhood, sexuality, education, poetry, television, poverty, or illness mean to other women, can offer feminists a way of replacing their presumptions of *a* female experience with a grounded sense of our commonalities and differences.

–Lila Abu-Lughod,
Can there be a feminist ethnography? (1990)

I have known "what it means to be a woman in other places and under different conditions." I was born and grew up in the Middle East, and have lived in the United States for a number of decades. These experiences embody the personal reasons for this paper. There are professional reasons as well. I have been interested in cross-cultural research issues throughout my professional career. Early in my career, I conducted research in Lebanon as part of a larger cross-cultural study of childrearing practices (Prothro & Diab, 1974). Later, I returned to explore the impact of culture upon interpersonal communication and helping behavior in a study of Lebanese and U.S. college students (Kikoski, 1980).

I returned again to Lebanon for my present research on feminist ethnography that seeks to understand the lifeworld of contemporary young women. I was myself an undergraduate in Lebanon, once the same age as the university women with whom I am conducting this research. I wondered how my story and that of my contemporaries might differ from theirs. It was these confluences and my curiosity about them that provided the impetus for this research.

To familiarize the reader with the area, this paper first will provide some historical and cultural context. While the region of the Arab Middle East may be referred to for context, the primary focus of this article is on Lebanon. Since this research is in progress, the reader is invited to share in these narratives and some preliminary reflections upon them.

LEBANON:
THE COUNTRY

Lebanon is a small country, almost the size of Connecticut, and located on the eastern shore (or Levant) of the Mediterranean. It is possible to find oneself in another country–Syria, Jordan, or Israel–if one drives more than two hours in any direction. Ancient home of the Phoenicians, its cosmopolitan people have lived for millennia at the rub point of Eastern and Western cultures. For centuries, the rugged mountains that rise sharply from a narrow coastal plain have provided refuge for minorities, most notably Christians after the Islamic conquest. Its geographic position, tradition of trade and commerce, and Christian population have generated more frequent contacts with the West than other parts of the Middle East. For centuries, France saw itself as the special protector of Lebanon's Christians. Even today, after Arabic, the tri-lingual Lebanese speak French perhaps more widely than English. The Western presence in an Arab country was broadened and deepened by the 19th century establishment of the American University of Beirut by American Presbyterian missionaries, as well as the founding of the Universite Saint-Joseph by French Jesuits. In addition to public educational institutions, many other American and European-affiliated schools and universities continue to educate large numbers of Lebanese.

Home to 16 officially-recognized religions and sects, Lebanon's political system is based on religious confessionalism–that is to say, according to religious communities. Political parties are largely but not exclusively organized along religious lines, and the legislature, as well as high administrative and elected positions are proportionately allocated by religion. Lebanon was (and remains) the only country in the Arab World where the President of the Republic must be Christian, the Prime Minister Sunni Moslem, and the Speaker of the Parliament Shi'ite Moslem. Long dominant in politics with more than 50 percent of the population, Lebanon's Christians today comprise about one-third of the population. It was this demographic shift that helped trigger the Lebanese Civil War. Lasting sixteen years, from 1975 to 1991, this civil war, like all civil wars, brought intense sufferings to the people. This long war shook the structure of Lebanese society and caused significant social change. In some instances, young women, some teenagers, fought on the front lines side-by-side with men. The chaos and crisis created a vacuum for Lebanese women to enter domains of society that the dominant patriarchal system had hitherto rendered inaccessible. Wars also created similar opportunities for women to participate in new ways in Iran in the 1980s, as well as in Kuwait and Saudi Arabia during the Gulf War (Yamani, 1996). Perhaps it takes a crisis, such as war, for those who hold power in patriarchal societies to discover that women can equally discharge the responsibilities of men–and are therefore entitled to equal rights.

PATRIARCHAL TRADITION AND ISLAM

To appreciate the cultural difficulties that confront Lebanese women, it is necessary to understand the larger context. The cultural backdrop of the Middle East is traditional, and much influenced by the conservatism of prevailing religions. It is important to note that Lebanon is part of a culture that is in transition more so than other Arab countries. Traditional cultures, irrespective of religions, tend to be patriarchal, to mute women's voices, and to place them into positions submissive to men. Religion also plays a very powerful and pervasive role in Middle Eastern society. Unique among Middle Eastern states, Lebanon has always had a substantial Christian population. Despite this large Christian population and Western presence, Lebanon is culturally and geographically part of the Arab world whose dominant faith is Islam.

Islam is a monotheistic religion that recognizes the unfolding revelation of Judaism in the Old Testament, and Christianity in the New Testament. But, according to Allah, and the Prophet Mohammed, the Koran is the final seal of divine revelation. Islam shares with Judaism and Christianity an ultimate belief in the individual's relationship with God. Upon death, Moslems believe in the judgment of individual souls by God, regardless of status, wealth, or gender. It is in this Divine recognition of the individual that Islamic feminists root their claim to equal treatment and an end to discrimination by males.

Islam is more than a religion in terms of a Westerner category of belief. It is an all-encompassing way of life. The Islamic tradition provides believers with guidance in areas of daily life that tends to govern their thoughts and actions. It provides its followers with a complete system of social conduct based on Divine sanction. (Berger 1964; Patai, 1983).

As is true of every religion, the texts of Islam have liberal and conservative interpreters. Islamic conservatives and fundamentalists might point out that the Koran states that females do not enjoy equal status with the male (Koran, Sura IV, verse 34). They also emphasize Koranic regulations in areas of marriage, divorce, and child custody that discriminate against women. They would also emphasize that in Islamic courts, women's testimony is valued at half that of males, as is the female Moslem's share of inheritance. Hence, Islamic beliefs buttress submissiveness and inequality in the status of women.

However, Islamic modernists and feminists might hold that Muhammad, as the Prophet of Allah, was a great reformer on behalf of women. He abolished the practice of female infanticide, and established women's rights to inherit and bequeath property, as well as to exercise control over their own wealth. Islam may be one of the only religions that has formally addressed women's rights, and sought to extend them. Islamic moderates and feminists emphasize that in Islam males and females are equal before God. Despite these differences of opinions, the conservative view generally has prevailed and been the norm. Women have far more circumscribed rights and roles than is true for women in the West. This gender sanction is not only religious, but linguistic as well. In Arabic there is no counterpart for the English word, child. A young human is either a boy (*walad*) or a girl (*bint*). In fact, the word for child and boy is the same (*walad*). When one asks in Arabic, "How many children do you have?" one is literally asking, "How many boys do you have?"

Patriarchal tradition and Islam together have created a Middle Eastern culture in which it is difficult for women to express yearnings for social equality, let alone realize them. Yet, advances continue as was manifested in the stories I heard from young Lebanese women.

CHILDREARING AND SOCIALIZATION IN THE MIDDLE EAST

Childrearing practices in the Middle East differ from those of the West. One of the fundamental differences is in attitudes toward independence and dependence. In the U.S., childrearing practices aim at socializing children from an early age to be independent. It is normally expected that by adolescence children will become partially independent by earning money at appropriate jobs. This was unheard of in the Middle East. Children are less likely to work or earn money until after graduation from college, although this may not be true in rural and poor areas. Such practices encourage more dependence in the Middle East, in comparison to the independence and autonomy fostered in the West.

In American society, one is raised to identify oneself as an individual, and only after as a member of one's family. In Middle Eastern society, one is raised to identify oneself with one's family and only after as an individual. Until recently in Arab society, one tended to identify oneself more with one's group, usually the extended family, than by one's personal identity, achievements, or status. In the Middle East, the basic objective of parents is to mold the child into an obedient, conforming group member so that individuals can easily integrate into their social environment.

Until recently, Middle Eastern childrearing also differed in the socialization of males and females. Males generally are favored over females even in infancy. Generally, females are weaned from the breast months and even years before males. The role for females that is prescribed by society and enforced by parents is to be more submissive and respectful than their male siblings. Females generally are granted less freedom in education, social behavior, work and other areas by the general norms of Middle Eastern society. Consequently, girls are rendered more dependent by socialization practices than are males.

I left the Middle East as a young woman over thirty years ago. At that time, women's voices still were muffled. That should come as no surprise given the existing cultural paradigm that we have reviewed. Yet, the struggle of these young women in Lebanon was not *ex nihilo*. Writers and activists had been raising women's consciousness and issues for more than a century.

ROOTS OF MIDDLE EASTERN FEMINISM

Some may be surprised to learn that feminism has a long history in the Middle East. The feminist movement began in Egypt toward the end of the 19th century, and rapidly spread. Women lobbied hard to enact changes in such areas as marriage, divorce, inheritance, and child custody laws, though they realized limited success. Historically, Moslem and Christian feminists of the 19th and 20th centuries have contributed in their own ways to making women's voices stronger.

Among these women was Aisha Ismat al-Taimuriya (1840-1902), an Egyptian feminist, who wrote fiery poetry against the veiling of women. Some scholars claim that she was the first among women or men to urge gender equality (Badran & Cooke, 1990; see also Nasrallah, 1986). Zainab Fawwaz (1860-1914), an erudite, self-taught Lebanese woman became a famous literary figure in both Beirut, Lebanon and Cairo, Egypt. In her poetry, Fawwaz rejected the veiling, and condemned the seclusion of women. Her writings supported women's rights to education, as well as to employment outside the home. In advocating women's right to work, she wrote: "Thus, we find that the markets are full of women vying with men in business transactions . . . the intelligent person who inquires into the affairs of this world finds the sexes equal" (Badran & Cooke, 1990; see also Nasrallah, 1986). Nazira Zain al-Din (1905- ?) was the Lebanese daughter of an Islamic scholar of religion and law who encouraged and guided her education. In her writings, and dialogues with clerics, she employed reason to criticize the practice of veiling: "I have noticed that the nations that have given up the veil are the nations that have advanced in intellectual and material life. Such advancement is not equaled in veiled nations" (Badran & Cooke, 1990).

Among the most fascinating Middle Eastern feminists is Egyptian writer, Huda Sha'raoui (1879-1947). As a young woman, she tossed away her veil, and led women's marches against the British colonial occupation of Egypt. She also fought to raise the legal age of marriage for young women from 13 to 16. What may be most significant is that she helped establish the Egyptian Feminist Union, which, in 1944, hosted the Arab Feminist Conference. Fifty-one resolutions emerged from this conference that addressed discrimination against women in social, political, and economic areas. Most astoundingly, one resolution addressed the problem of sexist language and called for the elimination of gender distinctions in Arabic, thus foreshadowing by decades similar efforts to address sexist language in English in the West (Badran & Cooke, 1990) At this conference, Lebanese educator Zahiya Dughan (n.d.) called for establishing chairs for women's studies departments in Arab colleges and universities. Further, she proposed that past and present literary, political and social contributions of Arab and Western women be collected and published in an Arab women's encyclopedia with these unifying words:

We in Lebanon, Syria, Iraq, and Egypt and other Arab countries should agree to a common plan for reviving our Arab heritage and adapting aspects of western culture, strengthening what is good in our heritage and borrowing what is good from Western culture . . . I believe this would be one of the most fruitful moves towards a unified future. (Badran & Cooke, 1990, pp. 341-42)

STATUS OF WOMEN IN THE MIDDLE EAST TODAY

Open discussion of feminist issues and women's advances toward legal equality gathered strength during the 19th and 20th centuries. During recent decades, the trend started to reverse as Islamic conservative movements spread and strengthened. For example, the 1979 establishment of an Islamic regime in Iran had a devastating effect on the status of women. Yet, during the post-revolution era, the voices of women began to be heard again. One of the most surprising voices was that of the Ayatollah Khomeni's daughter, Zahra Moustafavi, professor of philosophy at the University of Teheran and president of the Iranian Women's Association. In her own words, she said:

Islam gives men and women equal rights. If a woman wants to work outside the home, Islamic law allows her to, but the obstacle is the man . . . There should be a revolution of women in the home. They must rebel against some men . . . If a woman is doing the same work as a man, she should enjoy the same salary and the same advantages. (Goodwin, 1994, p. 119)

While Zahra Moustafavi could forcefully speak on behalf of women, not every woman in Iran has the position and privilege to voice her beliefs. However, the good news is that feminism in Iran lives despite the fact that it has been driven underground.

Most recently, the *New York Times* carried an op-ed article "Lipstick Politics in Iran" describing the defiant struggle of women in Iran who have become a "vibrant political force . . . (who) . . . have successfully invaded male territories, although a dab of lipstick can still land them in jail." The writer explains, "Lipstick is not just lipstick in Iran. It transmits political messages. It is a weapon" (Milani, 1999). After decades under the most conservative regime, feminist ideals not only persist but find a voice. In the 1997 Iranian national election, the women's vote was courted by and crucial to the victory of President Mohammad Khatami.

As a traditional society in transition, the status of women in the Middle East has been oscillating. Egypt was the first Arab country to educate women in the 1880s, and the first to establish a feminist movement in the 1920s. Yet, in 1979, two laws oppressive to women were passed in Egypt. The "Law of Obedience" required a wife to totally submit to the authority of her husband. The "Law of Return" compelled police to forcibly return a woman to her husband even though he had physically abused her. In March, 2000, Egyptian divorce laws were revised to give women equal rights to divorce their husbands. In addition, "honor killing," the practice of killing young women suspected of rape or sexual misbehavior, by family members still occurs, especially in tightly-knit, rural communities. Recently, in an audience with Queen Noor Al-Hussein, I was told of her successful efforts, with the support of her recently deceased husband, King Hussein, to make the honor killing of women a crime in Jordan (Queen Noor Al-Hussein, 1999).

In addition, the feminist movement in Arab countries is struggling to establish women's right to divorce, and to prevent divorce outside a court of law–as demanded in 1944 by the Arab Feminist Conference in Cairo. Since then some important reforms have taken place. In the past, a man could divorce his wife outside of court by repeating three times the words "I divorce you." Since 1960, an Egyptian husband demanding a divorce has had to state to the court his reason for it (Barakat, 1985).

There has been slow but steady increase in self-awareness among women in the Middle East today. For, as one observer put it: "When it comes to women's rights, religion and theology are invoked . . . Change is so difficult, because in Islam, women symbolize tradition and cultural identity. It is as if the whole burden of the Islamic tradition rests on their shoulders" (Simons, 1998).

Generalizations about the Middle East are not necessarily true of Lebanon. The status of women in the 1990s has improved, particularly over the past three decades. Women comprise 37 percent of the Lebanese labor force. This includes 14% of physicians, 17% of dentists, 20% of lawyers and 27% of pharmacists. But there remains a glass ceiling between most women in the workforce and top positions. Women are severely underrepresented in the upper, decision-making reaches of business, civil service, academia, and especially elective office. Women still have a long distance to go, yet are sustaining their efforts to move forward (Makdisi, 1996)

REFLECTIONS ON CURRENT ETHNOGRAPHIC RESEARCH IN LEBANON

In the late 1990s, I began a research project of interviewing Lebanese women in an effort to understand their views and perspectives on being a woman in contemporary Lebanon. These young women volunteered to take part in my research study on feminist ethnography in the Middle East on their college campus. They represented a spectrum of the religions and regions of Lebanon, and were mainly but not exclusively from middle class families.

For this exploratory research, I utilized ethnographic methodology that values discourse in culturally embedded contexts. I listened to young women's stories in an attempt to make meaning of their subjective experiences. As a researcher familiar with that culture, my goal was to understand these narratives from their positions in their own environment. In my interviews, I sought to hold to Steiner Kvale's position that the researcher needs to listen to what individuals convey about their lived world from their own point of view. I tried to understand the world from the narrator's special position. Using a semi-structured, informal conversational format, I tried to draw out each woman's story about everyday life including family and career, dreams, hopes, and fears (Kvale, 1996).

Recently, feminist ethnography has become a favored approach for researchers who, as Abu-Lughod stated, seek "to bring to life what it means to be a woman" in other places and cultures. This was my goal for this research.

Early on in my project, as I listened to these stories, I began to realize that they differed significantly from women's stories of past generations, even my own. Having grown up in that part of the world, and being myself a student in the same collegiate setting just a few decades earlier, I realized that profound change in these young women's perspectives had taken place. As their narratives unfolded, I was particularly struck by the differences in their views with those that I remembered from my own generational cohort.

In the next section of this paper, I will address the themes that emerged from these women's stories. The identification of themes emerged from the text of the interview. The purpose of my questions was to facilitate and thicken the natural flow of the narrative. According to Van Maanen, a thick description is a "written representation of a culture" (Van Maanen, 1988). It culturally situates the experience, and conveys the thoughts and meanings that undergird the experience as a process. Hence, the interviewer made use of open-ended questions to encourage and deepen the conversation. Every effort was made to respect the narrator's voice in the storying so that intrinsic themes could surface. The following section will treat these themes. Direct quotations from the stories are used to enable the reader to hear these women's voices. To protect the anonymity of these young women, their names have been changed.

CONTEXTUAL THEMES

Gender Equality

Forging new identities for themselves, these young Lebanese women are seeking equality and self-determination in their personal lives. In this process, they are creating a new stance for themselves that differs from the traditional stance of their parents.

Here, Rania told me her story about gender equality. As a young girl she was allowed to play with young boys until about age 10, when it became forbidden. As an adolescent, Rania, like other young women, was more restricted than her brothers whose curfews were far more lenient. As her brothers grew older, their freedom became more extended, while Rania's freedom was more tightly circumscribed.

Yet, Rania did not believe or practice the cultural inequality with which she was raised. She emphatically told me: "I feel that women are equal to men and sometimes even smarter. I see no reason for them not to have the same rights. My experience at the university is that women excel. They get higher grades, higher scores on standardized tests. They ought to have equal rights, total rights."

It is remarkable that an Arab feminist born in 1931 remembered similar experiences that triggered changes in her attitudes. Nawal al-Saadawi wrote: "I became a feminist when I was a child. Starting to feel the discrimination between myself and my brother, and how he was treated, how he had more privileges than I. I did very well at school. He did not. But over the summer holiday, he was rewarded by being allowed to travel and I was rewarded with nothing. So for me, it was really a lot of injustice. It started unconsciously when I was a child. I felt the discrimination. . . . I felt that my brother was privileged. And then when I grew up and I became a physician and I worked in rural areas I started to become aware of the fact that what I had felt years earlier was the truth. And that is how I became a feminist" (Badran & Cooke, 1990).

Rima, age 19 and a college sophomore, told me about her views on gender equality. "All four girls in my family are bright. My father was very harsh on my brother, but he was proud of his daughters and their accomplishments. My parents did not favor my brother, who is the only male child, yet my grandmothers did. My parents didn't think less of their girls, they thought of all their children equally." The stories of these two young women illustrate the generational shifts in perspectives that have occurred on gender equality in their families.

Suha sees some change in the relationships between the genders: "In general, I see men still wanting to dominate women, though it is beginning to change. More and more men my age see us as equals. In the past, when you went out on a date, he had to pay your way. But today, many feel that they can go 'Dutch,' and pay their own ways." Just few decades ago, a young women paying her share of a date was unheard of in Lebanon.

Through these young women, we hear stories of change embedded in personal lives, families and generations.

Independence/Autonomy

Until very recently, the cultural expectation was for young women in Lebanon to live with their parents until marriage. Nuha, age 21, holds different beliefs. She explains that upon completion of her studies, she sees herself moving away from home to wherever her job takes her. She continues: "I expect to support myself through my career. I should be responsible for myself. My parents sacrificed a lot to educate me, and now I need to be self-reliant and independent. While my parents expect me to work, they probably would not want me to move out of the house and live on my own. I see it differently. I need to be independent and begin to live my own life."

Mariam, a recent graduate who is employed by the university, told a different story about autonomy: "When I recently took this job, after I returned from study abroad, I had to convince my parents to let me share an apartment with a friend. Now that I live on my own, my parents do not mind it." She went on: "I do not want to compare men with women. A woman can do anything she wants nowadays. The only difference between a man and a woman is that she can conceive, and he can't. Woman can do anything they want. My perspective is that I like to share everything, all the responsibilities, with my boyfriend. If we marry someday, I wouldn't expect him to buy me a house. I work and I earn money as well. I do not want to have to wait for a man to offer me things. We can share. There shouldn't be a power structure in our relationship."

Twenty-year old Nada, who comes from a more conservative home, is struggling with her new thoughts and identity: "I would like to have the freedom to make my own decisions. However, there is also tradition in our culture, and sometimes I have difficulties going against it. Though, when I am right, I would do the impossible to follow through on it." For many young women, this struggle is real. They find themselves reaching to become independent and emancipated, while they feel the strong pull of cultural imperatives through their families. Yet what comes across is the awareness that these women have their commitment to their values, and their courage to begin to address these issues. This is in itself a remarkable change.

Career

Most of these women seem to have a strikingly emancipated view of career. Most of their stories told of their determination to have a career after graduation. Rola shared her dreams of a career in the field of social work. She hopes to continue work after marriage, whenever it happens. Surprisingly, she did not talk about marriage before career. This appears to be a new trend in the thinking of these young women who now are more concerned about their personal independence and autonomy. Such an attitude marks a departure from the cultural expectations that prevailed when I was a student in Lebanon, and even differs from the pre-Civil War era. When asked what she would like to do following her graduation from college, Rola said: "As soon as I complete my education, I will begin searching for a job. I certainly am not getting an education to sit home. I am studying Interior Design, and that's what I intend to do as a professional."

On the topic of career, Rima stated: "In my family, we girls were encouraged to attend the university and choose our own majors. No one in the family tried to influence our choices. My parents wanted us to make our own decisions. I chose to study fine arts even though to work within my field may not be possible now.

I studied it because of my love for the arts. To be realistic, I may not find a position in this field, yet I am willing to work in a related field like advertising or something like that. I certainly will keep up with that interest in my free time. My commitment is to have a career, and to support myself by earning a living." She went on: "A woman shouldn't stay at home. She needs to grow and evolve. I hope to marry someone who shares my views and thinking. The rules should not be different for him and me."

Rima goes on to say: "Lebanese women still have not achieved their full rights. Women still are not perceived as being capable of doing what they actually can do. For instance, women are still not allowed to serve in the army, though we are capable of doing so. I would like to change that. I would very much like to join the army."

She went on to talk about the social perception of women professionals: "Even though women are excelling in their careers as doctors, for example, the perception is that men make better doctors. I resent it when some of my friends say things like that, and I correct them."

These stories resonated with the themes of personal independence and individual careers. These issues possess an importance to these women that was not as true in earlier decades. They seem to be propelling these young women's efforts to forge their own identities.

Marriage

The topic of marriage surfaced in every story. It was not too long ago when arranged marriages were the norm. They still are common in some strata of Lebanese society. Furthermore, marriages between cousins, even first cousins, still occur in some communities. To my surprise, none of these women even entertained such thoughts.

Regardless of the community or home in which they grew up, these women voiced an ardent desire to meet their future partners on their own, rather than through arranged circumstances. These women placed a high priority upon synchronicity with their mates in values, expectations, outlooks and ideals. Hence, the traditional approaches to meeting and getting to know their partners are no longer fitting for them. These new trends are gaining impetus in this transitional society. I see the determination and courage of these individual young women as a genesis of social change.

Rania, who is 20 years old, is typical. Her father wants to know not only about her boyfriend's family and level of education, but, in particular, about his religion. Rania's response to him was: "It does not matter. Family and religion are to be dealt with only by the concerned individuals." What is important to Rania is that the two young adults share similar ideals and values. When asked how she would resolve her differences with her parents, Rania cites the power of persuasion through dialogue with her parents: "It is something that I will continue to deal with in order to arrive at a mutually acceptable resolution. I do not believe in family dissension. My family is important to me, and I cherish these relationships. But my life is my own."

Lebanese law does not recognize inter-religious marriages. These marriages still are one of the deepest taboos in Lebanese society. This was hardly the case in the narratives I heard. Mona, a Maronite Christian, told me: "My parents and grandparents wouldn't want me to marry outside my religion. For them, inter-religious marriage is out of the question. But they don't know that I am in love with a Shi'ite (Moslem). All of my friends are of different faiths. I have friends who are Jews, Christians, Moslems, and my parents know that. My mother has made it clear to me that she doesn't want me to go out with my Shi'ite boyfriend. But she doesn't know that I am in love with him. This mentality is difficult for me. It is taboo to marry outside one's religion. But in my view, what matters is the quality of the person." For Mona and others like her, interfaith marriages create conflicts. Alienating the family is not an option. While they have the power of personal conviction, these women opt to delay marriage while they work to resolve such issues. Mona stated: "I do not want to upset my family. I want to take the time. I will probably talk to my mother first, and try to convince her. Then I hope that my mother can convince my father. This is a real dilemma for me." On the issue of career and marriage, Dima had her own views: "I see no problem with being married and having a career. I believe that husband and wife should help each other. A man should support his wife if she chooses to have a career. I don't think that a man has the right to interfere in his wife's decision to work outside the home. Men have to respect women and their rights."

The stories that I heard reflect a new sense of women's position in Lebanese society. The power of their convictions amazes and astounds me. They are free-thinking women who have arrived at these perspectives with few actual role models. They have achieved this stance in a society that is generally less supportive of such aspirations and attitudes.

Childrearing and Career

On the issue of raising a family while maintaining a career, these young women, once again, have their own unique views that certainly differ from those of their parents. These views are congruent with their own values of independence and autonomy. Dima's story is not unique. When she spoke of raising a family, Dima stated: "I may have to adjust my work schedule to be with my children, and work at the same time. That is what my older sister already does. Her children go to a nursery for part of the day. I believe it is important to raise one's children, and simultaneously to have a career."

Suha had a slightly different view on childrearing: "When the children are small, I will probably stay home with them. I do not believe in placing young children in daycare. Then, when they are older, I will go back to my job." She goes on to address the reason why she wants to be involved in the upbringing of her children: "I want to raise my own children with egalitarian ideas. I will raise my sons and daughters as equals. This is how my generation can begin to change the next generation. Boys and girls should be able to do the same things. They are equally capable."

Maha hopes to work out joint career plans and shared childcare schedules with her future husband. The idea here is for both of them to maintain their careers while raising their young family. This probably was the most unexpected theme to surface. As the story further unfolded, I heard a profound yearning for equality with their male counterparts. These women have a vision of themselves as being entitled to share childcare with their partners. In Maha's view, these issues ought to be negotiated and agreed upon even prior to marriage. Such attitudes mark a sharp departure from the clearly defined gender roles and childcare practices that are characteristic of traditional societies, particularly in the Middle East.

Once again, this affirmed for me the determination of these young women to no longer be subservient to the dominance of the male. They see their relationships with their partners as based on equality and collaboration. Such a shift in values may require changes in the mores of the culture. They want to ensure that their children embrace these values in order to change future generations.

CONCLUDING REFLECTIONS

There is a long and deeply rooted history of feminism in the Middle East. The road that it has traveled has been arduous, given the terrain it has traversed. Patriarchal tradition and the conservatism of prevailing religion in the region have meant that women's struggle for emancipation and equality has had to be fought on many different levels.

Some movement toward progress is being felt throughout the region as a deeper awareness of women's rights takes hold. Women in different Arab countries and societies are seizing the opportunity to push their agenda forward.

Perhaps the greatest gain has taken place in young women's self-awareness. This was reflected in the narratives that I was privileged to hear during my interviews with them. A number of themes repeatedly surfaced in these young women's stories.

These young women have a clear vision of themselves in their society, and the role they must play to realize that vision. They place a high value on safeguarding their relationships within their own families. They are willing to struggle for the right to meet and choose a partner whose values are synchronous with their own. These women place a high value upon their own career because, as one woman put it, a woman "needs to grow and evolve." But not at the price of motherhood or children. Motherhood is very important. These women are willing to temporarily sacrifice their careers out of concern for their children's welfare. They also plan to raise their children and have richer marriages because of the more egalitarian and collaborative values that will suffuse these relationships. After such a terrible civil war, their willingness to put aside religion as a factor in an individual's worth leads one to marvel at the wisdom of the young, and to hope for the future.

These young women maintain one foot in one of the most traditional societies, and the other in a modern world of their own creation. This seems to be possible because of the clear-minded, mature pragmatism by which these young women have decided to live their lives, and the personal strength with which they already have begun to do so. These women appear to have arrived at these powerful convictions as a result of their own independent logic and critical thinking. Their hope is to lead more autonomous lives, but not at the price of the relationships that sustain and nourish them.

The overarching theme of this research seems to be the universal yearning of women to be free to express themselves, and to realize their goals and dreams in their own ways and in their own cultural contexts. This is a universal yearning among women in all cultures. Perhaps, only by being grounded in each culture's feminism can we see feminism's universality. There is a history of feminism that is rooted in the Middle East. And there is a future.

REFERENCES

Abu-Lughod, L. (1990). Can there be a feminist ethnography? In *Women & Performance Project at the Department of Performance Studies,* New York: University/ Tisch School of the Arts.

Al-Hussein, Queen Noor. (March 4, 1999). Audience, Delegation of Arab-American Women. Amman, Jordan: Bab Al-Salam Palace.

Badran, M. & Cooke, M. (1990). In M. Badran & M. Cooke (Eds.). *Opening the Gates: A Century of Arab Feminist Writing.* Bloomington & Indianapolis: Indiana University Press.

Barakat, H. (1985). The Arab family and the challenge of social transformation. In E. W. Fernea (Ed.). *Women and the Family in the Middle East.* Austin: University of Texas Press.

Berger, M. (1964). *The Arab World Today.* Garden City: Doubleday & Co.

Goodwin, J. (1994*). Price of Honor: Muslim Women Lift the Veil of Silence on the Islamic World.* Boston/New York: Little Brown and Company.

Kikoski, C. K (1980). A study of cross-cultural communication, Arabs and Americans: paradigms and skills. *Unpublished doctoral dissertation.* University of Massachusetts, Amherst.

Kvale, S. (1996). *Inter Views: An introduction to qualitative interviewing.* Thousand Oaks: Sage Publications.

Makdisi, J.S. (1996). The mythology of modernity: women and democracy in Lebanon. In M. Yamani (Ed.*). Feminism and Islam: Legal and Literary Perspectives.* New York: New York University Press.

Milani, F. (August 19,1999). *Lipstick politics in Iran.* New York Times.

Nasrallah, E. (1986). *Women Pioneers* (in Arabic). Beirut: Muassassat Nawfal.

Patai, R. (1973). *The Arab Mind.* New York: Charles Scribner & Sons.

Prothro, E. T. & Diab, L. (1974). *Changing Family Patterns in the Arab World.* Beirut: American University of Beirut.

Simons, M. (March 9, 1998*). Cry of Muslim women for equal rights is rising.* New York Times.

Van Maanen, J. (1988). *Tales of the field: On writing ethnography.* Chicago: University of Chicago Press.

Yamani, M. (1996). Introduction. In Yamani, Mai. (Ed.*). Feminism and Islam: Legal and Literary Perspectives.* New York: New York University Press.

INTERVIEWS

Catherine Weigel Foy, Interview Editor

An Interview with Janine Roberts

Janine Roberts, EdD, is Professor in the School of Education, Counseling and Social Justice Programs at the University of Massachusetts in Amherst, where she teaches, conducts research, and supervises clinical work.
　　The author of a recently released book, *Tales and Transformations* (Norton Press), and co-author of *Rituals for Our Times* (Jason Aronson Press), she is perhaps best known for her contributions in the areas of training and supervision, family rituals and stories, and gender and multiculturalism in family therapy. She is the most recent past editor of the *Journal of Feminist Family Therapy,* and has served on the editorial boards of the major family

---

Catherine Weigel Foy, MSW, is Associate Director of Graduate Education at The Family Institute of Northwestern University, and Lecturer in the School of Education and Social Policy, Northwestern University, 618 Library Place, Evanston, IL 60201.

　　[Haworth co-indexing entry note]: "An Interview with Janine Roberts." Foy, Catherine Weigel. Co-published simultaneously in *Journal of Feminist Family Therapy* (The Haworth Press, Inc.) Vol. 11, No. 4, 2000, pp. 147-157; and: *Feminism, Community, and Communication* (ed: Mary E. Olson) The Haworth Press, Inc., 2000, pp. 147-157. Single or multiple copies of this article are available for a fee from The Haworth Document Delivery Service [1-800-342-9678, 9:00 a.m. - 5:00 p.m. (EST). E-mail address: getinfo@haworthpressinc com].

　　　　　　© 2000 by The Haworth Press, Inc. All rights reserved.

therapy journals. She had held board positions in both the American Family Therapy Academy, and the American Association for Marriage and Family Therapy. This interview was conducted on August 19, 1999.

CF: You've worked in the field of marriage and family therapy for several decades, have contributed to the field as a trainer, supervisor, teacher, therapist, writer–I don't know if it's in that order–but certainly all of those things and probably a few more. Can we begin by talking about how long you've been in the field and how you got into it?

JR: I've been in the field for about 25 years. I got into it in this way. I was hired to set up a community school in Philadelphia–a small parent co-op school (that actually still exists). Mostly women were on the parent board; it was this group of women who wanted to have a racially mixed school in a school district which, at that time, had very few racially mixed schools. It was in the early seventies. I worked a lot with the families–every family had to put in "x" number of hours in the school.

CF: Sounds similar to the current charter school movement.

JR: Yes, there were a lot of alternative schools at that point. I knew that when we worked well with families as part of the school community and when we had a good connection with them that it really made a difference for the kids. It also helped if I understood some of the dynamics and knew where the kids were coming from. So I started going to the Eastern Pennsylvania Psychiatric Institute to take a once-a-month seminar on family therapy; they lent out books and videotapes for free to anybody in the community. And that's where I started with people like Uri Rueveni. He did a lot of work with network therapy. Nobody talks much about that work now but it certainly had implications for feminist family therapy. Ivan Boszormenyi-Nagy and Geraldine Sparks were there also.

CF: That's right.

JR: So, that's where I got really intrigued. I could see how useful the family therapy concepts were in thinking about very intricate interactions and understanding schools as a system, the family system, and the interface between the two.

But my interest goes back further than that in the sense that I came of age as the women's movement was just starting. I really credit the women's movement in my teenage years for giving me a platform for even thinking about having a career. Women in my immediate family didn't have access to higher education. My sister and I both

	were first generation female college graduates (my father had a college education).
CF:	So your interests in women's issues and in the family were intertwined at an early age.
JR:	And also, the fact that my family moved to Kuwait when I was sixteen–that had a big impact. That was 1963. I lived in Kuwait and then I lived in Beirut. I went to a boarding school. Seeing the United States from the perspective of other countries both made me more aware of some of our shortcomings but at the same time appreciative of what was possible for women. It was so different living in the Middle East at that point in time and certainly changed my life.
CF:	Were you free to come and go and dress as you wished?
JR:	No. I basically could not go out alone. If I went into the marketplace, the big souk, which was primarily men at that point, I always wore long sleeves and long dresses. I didn't actually put on a veil. Once in a while I might wear it if I were going out of the city, but if I went in the souk, my father had to walk in front of me and my brother behind me or I would get pinched and fondled pretty badly.
CF:	That was quite an experience. Multiculturalism informed your experience early on.
JR:	It did. But at the same time Kuwait was starting schools for girls. They were rapidly making opportunities available for women. So, it was a fascinating contrast.
CF:	And then you came back to the states for college?
JR:	I came back actually for my senior year in high school. Another very informative experience was my time in VISTA. I was in one of the first groups trained in the domestic peace corps. It had just started in 1965 and I joined them after I graduated from high school. I grew up in rural Washington state. I was so isolated, and going overseas to Kuwait really opened up a new world to me. My brother and I came back via the east coast and spent some time in New York. Then I took the Greyhound bus across the U.S. from New York City. I realized that the east coast was so different from the west coast and I wanted to get back to the east coast somehow. I didn't really have money for private schools or even state schools. So, I thought "Well, I'll do VISTA." And I asked them to send me to the east coast and they sent me to Newark. Newark had a big SDS (Students for a Democratic Society) and a big SNCC (Student Non-violent Coordinating Committee) project there. So the government was sending in these VISTA people to try to counteract their projects. So that was

CF: also a very informative time in trying to think about issues of inclusivity and oppression within the society. I was living in high rise public housing in Newark.

CF: And after that, you went back to school then?

JR: Yes. I went to Rutgers in Newark, and then to an institute in Argentina for a semester. And then I went back to the University of Washington and finished up there.

CF: A great globe-trotting experience! And certainly informing how you looked at the United States experience of growing up.

JR: Oh, absolutely! I think it influenced my work as an editor of the *Journal of Feminist Family Therapy,* too. When I was editor we switched over the name of the journal and added the subtitle "An International Forum." I worked to get women from other countries on the board and to have a more diverse representation of women within the U.S. as well. I think this also grew out of the conference in Copenhagen that Monica McGoldrick and Betty Carter and Evan Imber-Black and other women organized.

CF: And that was the women's conference?

JR: Yes. That was the International Women's Conference. One was done in Connecticut earlier, which was more for U.S. women. But the Copenhagen one was an international one and they got a powerful group of women from all over. It was a wonderful conference. It was very much "let's find out where we're at in all these different countries and how we can support each other and what kind of network can we build." In the last issue of *JFFT* that Lois Broverman edited before she stepped down and I took over, she actually published quite a few things from that conference. This was a great segue and launch into having a more international focus. This is not easy when the journal is in English and published here and people don't have access to it overseas. There are all kinds of political problems with it.

CF: Did the readership of the journal then expand to include more of an international base?

JR: It has somewhat but it's really a problem in terms of people having access to paying in U.S. funds and getting it.

CF: I'm going to switch back to some of your earlier work, if we can for a minute. As a therapist in postgraduate training here in Chicago, I was very struck by your earliest writings. These writings were on supervision and the use of the team approach, published in the *Journal of Strategic and Systemic Therapy.*

JR: Yes, long ago.

CF: What struck me about that was the feminist stance you took regarding the supervisory relationship. You really advocated more of the flattening out of the hierarchy in supervision. Back in the early eighties that was quite a switch to make and I was wondering what kind of response you received from these publications?

JR: Well, I think the field was just on the cusp of thinking about more collaborative relationships both in therapy and in training. So it was generally pretty positive. I think people were trying to move away from the sense that the supervisor/trainer always knows best–that the supervisor will walk in the room and show you how it's really done. For my dissertation, I was interviewing Minuchin and asked him, "Do you think it ever undermines trainees when you walk into the room and say how you should do this and how you should do that and then walk out again?" He said, "No. Because that's how hierarchy works, and everybody recognizes that." I thought to myself, you might see it differently depending on your world view.

CF: Yes, then you did some research on that very question, right?

JR: Yes. That's what I did my dissertation on. The thing that I find interesting in thinking about my career is that it's all there–many of the issues feminism has dealt with. But at times I did not link them to feminist theory. I have always been somewhat wary of jargon and like to stick close to our daily lived experiences.

CF: That's interesting because I was very struck by the theme of feminism that has threaded through all of your work. You also advocated for more of a team or collaborative approach when you wrote your book on rituals, co-edited with Evan Imber-Black and Richard Whiting.

JR: I think that book marked a turning point. Some of my earliest work was about a more collaborative approach in training and that seeped into more of the therapy work. When Evan Imber-Black and I did the book, *Rituals for Our Times,* it was written for everyday people and therapists. I think that makes even more of a statement. The Milan group did work on rituals which very much focused on the therapist knowing the best rituals for the family.

CF: It put the responsibility on the therapist to come up with some magic moment.

JR: And as we talked with families and the more we worked with families around rituals, they shared all kinds of creative rituals in their daily lives that were already helping them to deal with the wide variety of family forms that they were in. Family therapy theory often has not kept up with changing family forms. And it was so much fun to write that book, *Rituals for Our Times,* tapping into all I had learned from clients and students in training, and hopefully helping family therapy theory move beyond its sometimes narrow focus on traditional families.

CF: Being familiar with (yet different than) the Milan approach set you up to follow the next great wave in the field of family therapy and that was the narrative approach.

JR: Yes. It was such a funny link, though. When you look at how the Milan work ended up going, the team split off into different directions and then the Milan Associates began what led to the current day narrative approach. When I did the book, *Tales and Transformations,* I was trying to locate myself in among those various strands.

CF: What really prompted you to tackle this?

JR: It was similar to the journey I took in the first book, *Rituals in Family Therapy,* with Evan and Dick Whiting. In the first chapter in that book I tried to do an overview of where everybody else was at– not only in the field of family therapy, but also in anthropology and the other disciplines. It was arduous. I did it because I think it helped me understand better what direction I was moving in. Whenever you have any chance to compare and contrast it gives you a backboard to push off against and see where you're positioned.

CF: That's right!

JR: But it wasn't nearly as much fun to write. Although the chapter on rituals and training was and the chapter I did with clients–a case study–that really taught me a lot about collaboration.

CF: That was the one about the psychiatric client. That was a very moving chapter.

JR: And, you know, I'm still in touch with that family. My daughter had her senior year violin recital and they attended. It was so sad because the husband had just died before that and the wife came. They had continued to do so well. Something shifted in our relationship once we wrote that chapter together. There weren't quite the same boundaries in terms of therapist and client relationship. We had boundaries, we were not friends, we don't hang out but when there are significant markers in either one of our lives we let each other know.

Anyway, to get back to my point, I think once I wrote *Rituals for Our Times,* writing was so much more invigorating. And I guess I was more comfortable writing that. So I was doing workshops on a lot of my ideas about stories and was thinking about cultural frames for stories and how to operationalize these. So much of the work on multicultural counseling talks about what you need to do without really showing you what it means to get inside and define the ideas. The book, *Tales and Transformations,* really grew out of the workshops and the teaching I was doing. We were just finishing up *Rituals for Our Times* and I was feeling kind of bereft. You know how at the end of a big project, you had all this energy focused on the project...

CF: And then face "now what?"

JR: I sat down and just started doing an outline for *Tales and Transformations* and somehow I was ready to do that book. It just sort of fell out. I sent it to Norton and they said, "Yes we're interested." That hasn't always been my experience. I was looking for a publisher last year for one on breast cancer and the family. I didn't find one.

CF: I'm surprised.

JR: Well, there are a lot of cancer books out there. They don't do very well. People don't like to buy cancer books.

CF: You know I was very moved by your writing in the *Family Therapy Networker* about your struggle with cancer. I thought you raised a lot of very good issues about how the professional and the personal aspects of our lives get kind of mushed up at times. We need to know how to manage that and how to use it for the benefit of the client. Your description was very moving.

JR: It was good to write that. It felt like I could let go of some parts of my experience, by getting it out there. Like "OK, that's got its place and I can move on."

CF: How do you think your feminism informed that experience?

JR: Well, there were a couple of interesting things. Most of my doctors throughout were women. And so these were women mostly younger than me who had the benefit of getting medical training because of the feminist movement. It was wonderful. I felt like I was in this webbing of women who had the possibility to be able to do that. So that was one whole piece of it. I think also my experiences with feminism and thinking about collaborative relationships gave me a place in which to feel like I had a right to speak up, negotiate, work directly with people and I felt people were very responsive to that.

CF: I remember a piece in your writing where you described that experience. The doctor had given his little spiel, about how he was going to do this, and then this would happen, and then you reached out your hand and said, "Hello."

JR: Yes. It's very fascinating in the medical world right now. All of these things that they do inform you about puts a lot more pressure on you –the patient–to be in charge of decisions. For example in breast cancer, there are a lot of points along the way where they will say. "Do you want this kind of treatment? Do you want chemo or radiation first?" I would think to myself I don't know! That part was fascinating. I don't see that prior generations have had that kind of power given to them in making major medical decisions. It felt both so invigorating and terrifying at the same time. I think it taught me a lot more about power and control issues. I wanted to have a say in my treatment because everything else was so out of control. At the same time, I felt the fear of having to make life and death kinds of decisions for myself. But it also gave me more respect for what it must mean to people in the medical profession, having to make these kind of decisions.

CF: Yes, the pressure to be up-to-date on the latest research published last week must be enormous. How do you think this whole experience has impacted your clinical work?

JR: Well, it certainly made me think even more carefully about when it's appropriate to share your life or stories with clients, what kind of guidelines we need to take into consideration, and, the responsibility we have to really have a very strong sense of where we stand in relationship to our own life experience so that we use it in the interests of the client. If we share a story from our personal life, it is essential that we don't have an agenda for how clients are going to respond to it and that we're not working through emotional reactions as we often do in telling and re-telling stories. You're not getting somebody's else's take on it so you can learn about your own emotions. There are such fine lines. How do we use our personal experience in a joining kind of way and not in a narcissistic kind of "now see me." This is an issue in teaching as well. Where is that line? Where can I share something that will be informative? It can be very reassuring to clients to share struggles you have faced because they know they're not alone. But it has to be presented in a way to highlight what the dilemmas and the challenges are, not just some simplistic–this is how I felt. If you do that, you are not giving them a road map, enough insight into what you struggled with so somebody else can latch onto some part of it.

CF: We need to look at it in terms of a process rather than as an answer.

CF: Well, moving back to our field, where do you think feminism is going? The thrust in the '80s was in critiquing the field, raising questions about the models, about practice. Where do you think it's going at this point?

JR: Oh, boy! I think the field of family therapy itself is having its own troubles with having a sense of identity. Too many people say "I do family therapy" and they don't necessarily have training in it. Managed care issues have intruded in on people. So few people can afford one-way mirrors and team training and supervision. I think family therapy in and of itself is suffering. I think it'll come back around again. I mean these things come and go.

I'm thinking out loud here. In terms of feminism, I hope one way it goes is that feminism continues to be infused with social justice issues more throughout treatment and training. I think social justice issues get dropped a lot of times because of the short length of treatment. I don't think we've come to a real integration of social justice issues with feminism and in therapy. It's not easy to do.

CF: That's true.

JR: It often gets lost in political frays that I don't think should be imposed on families. I'm at a place in my career where I ask how do I find out more from families about how they have dealt with social justice issues in the same way that I asked families about rituals. Families informed me and took me in another direction.

CF: It's a very sensitive issue to deal with, I think, especially for beginning therapists. It really takes quite a bit of finesse.

JR: Yes, there is no way you can impose your agenda on what you think they should be attentive to around prejudice, discrimination, oppression, whatever. On the other hand, if you don't find some way to ask about and bring them up, it leaves the family with no way to negotiate with each other or give voice to something that maybe has not been named. For example, I was working with a family two months ago. There is a biological child, a teenager, who's half African American and Jewish. She has no contact with her father. For various reasons, there's a cut-off there. The child is being raised in a primarily Jewish family, and has some real issues in junior high, about what groups she fits into and about whether her mother was trying to control how she dresses, so she doesn't get into the wrong crowd. So I ask, "What does it mean that you are biracial? Do you see yourself as different?" I wonder how do I have a discussion that opens it up.

She says, "It's something we never talk about at home. I do feel different. I would like to talk about it because I think it would make me feel more connected." To be able to talk about some of the experiences she's had around prejudice at school is helpful. But it's almost easier to talk about those experiences than it is to talk about "Who am I in this family?" The question is how do you bring this up in a way that's facilitative.

CF: Well, certainly that is a trend that Monica McGoldrick has addressed as well as others and I certainly hope that that continues. What other trends do you see in the field that we need to or maybe we hope to get to in the future?

JR: Well, this is an idiosyncratic interest. I think it is important to consider ways we can integrate the arts in thinking about psychological theory; novelists and playwrights are often ahead of us in the same way families are often ahead of us.

JR: One of the books I'm using right now in teaching is called *Monkey Bridge* by a Vietnamese American woman, Lan Cao. It has vibrant explications of multigenerational processes. You finish that book and you have some sense of the issues and struggles that each generation faced with migration to the U.S. and how that informs the relationship between generations. We need to access the materials that are out there. Another good example is Eva Hoffman's *Lost in Translation,* which is a memoir of her move from Poland to Vancouver, Canada and then to the U.S. Her focus on language is very applicable to therapeutic process because, as therapists we need to be thinking about what it means to be working in one language when your client's primary language is another language. What does it mean to have someone translating for someone else? What does it mean for you to hear something that's been translated, but to have access to the non-verbals of the person in the room? Some of the materials that we have to depend on as family therapists when we think about intricate processes, about change over time in families, about the whole context in which families live, are captured by novelists and memoirists.

CF: It really humanizes our theory.

JR: I'm sure I'm drawn to it partly because I like to use every day language when I talk about complex human interactions. The novelists do it so well. I really don't like using diagnostic language.

CF: For family therapists, that is a comfortable position.

JR: Yes. It is.

CF:	Is there anything else you would like to add about the field, about future trends?
JR:	I hope the field gets back to having a sense of history, and identity-what it stands for. Maybe some of this can come from work with social justice issues. There have been so many guild issues that have intruded on the field itself. Some of the vision and foresight has been lost in the struggle to stay afloat.
CF:	Yes, much energy has been spent elsewhere. The theme that has come through all of your work is collaboration and this interview has been a very collaborative process. I have enjoyed interviewing you. I hope we can meet in person some day.
JR:	I would love to.

BOOK REVIEWS

Anne C. Bernstein, Book Review Editor

LATINO FAMILIES IN THERAPY: A GUIDE TO MULTICULTURAL PRACTICE. By Celia Jaes Falicov. *New York: Guilford Press, 1998, 303 pp., $32.*

The attempt to provide culturally-sensitive mental health care has led to the emergence of two troubling trends in our field. First, there is a tendency to train mental health providers working with multicultural populations by giving them the "highlights" of the culture and immigration experience of prevalent minority groups (e.g., Latino, West Indian, Chinese, etc.). These ethnographic descriptions often become the stereotypes through which clinicians see or describe their patients. This approach frequently interferes with, or delays, the therapeutic alliance, and the tendency of even leading therapists to ignore unwittingly the nuances of each patient's experience too often results in patients feeling misunderstood.

Second, many mental health institutions place an emphasis on "ethnic matching" between patients and therapists, which encourages therapists to treat patients whose ethnic background is similar to their own or whose first language is the same. The assumption is that such therapists have a privileged understanding of these patients' experiences and are automatically qualified to treat them. This does not take into account how varied and multifaceted the immigration experience in the United States really is. In her book, *Latino Families in Therapy: A Guide to Multicultural Practice,* Celia Jaes Falicov takes issue with these widespread practices, which she sees as more limiting than helpful, and presents an alternative approach to treating multicultural families.

As Falicov states in her introduction, "deciding how, when, and even why to introduce cultural and sociopolitical contexts in therapy is a difficult but necessary task." She proceeds to argue eloquently for the need to make cultural sensitivity an integral aspect of therapeutic training and treatment at all levels. To this end, she developed the "Multidimensional Ecosystemic Comparative Approach (MECA)," which she describes as a "cultural generalist" framework which can be employed with clients from any cultural background. Through MECA, Falicov aims to provide the means for therapists to explore the similarities and differences between their culture and that of their clients so as to enable therapists to understand more accurately their clients' problems, needs, and resources.

The book proposes an expanded framework for the understanding of the individuals and families we treat, one that moves away from the unidimensional view of "culture as ethnicity" framework to a more multifaceted definition of culture. MECA is based on the premise that each person's cultural identity is really an "ecological niche" made up of the multitude of cultural contexts in which the person is embedded. These include race, social class, religion, occupation, language, and cohort. Given this broad definition of culture, it becomes increasingly clear that static ethnic descriptions, which are supposed to apply to a whole ethnic group, would not accurately portray the situation of a given family or person. Moreover, Falicov proposes that we can all find points of contact ("cultural borderlands") with our clients. For example, while we may not share the same ethnicity, we may share the experience of migration, or have a similar educational or socioeconomic level.

Falicov champions the taking of an exploratory stance to avoid stereotyping families and their concerns. She stresses that therapists working with immigrant families should obtain an overview of the family's situation and conduct an in-depth investigation of the family's migration history within the first couple of sessions. This facilitates making decisions regarding areas for further inquiry and treatment planning and helps in uncovering cultural cues to particular presenting problems or symptoms-cues which generally will be useful in the therapist's collaborating with the family to find creative, culturally-congruent solutions. However, Falicov recognizes that a purely free-form approach may leave therapists lost and floundering amidst an enormous amount of cultural information. Her model is an attempt to provide a solution in the form of a useful therapeutic frame aimed at obtaining a balance between maintaining an "attitude of curiosity" and efficiently gathering the information relevant to the therapeutic process.

To this end, she devised four "generic cultural domains" which provide a map for the therapist to explore together with the family. The first domain, "the journey of migration and culture change," deals with variations in "when, why, and how a family came to migrate," paying close attention to the motivation for migration and the adaptation to the host culture for the family as a whole and for each of its members. The second domain, "ecological context," looks at the family's living environment– communities, support systems, working conditions, and involvement with schools and social agencies. It includes aspects such as race and racism and religious and health belief systems, sensitizing therapists to the psychological effects of marginalization. The third generic domain is that of "family organization," through which cultural variations in family structure and the values attached to them are examined. The fourth and last domain is that of the "family life cycle," which explores the cultural patterns in family developmental stages and transitions, such as the expectations of children's and adolescents' behavior.

After presenting the basics of MECA, the remainder of the book is organized into four sections, each of which elaborates on one of the generic domains in the model. Through these in-depth discussions of the many facets of immigrant experience, Falicov fosters therapists' awareness of what to look for when exploring these domains with patients. She includes the brief migration histories of three Latino groups: Mexicans, Puerto Ricans, and Cubans; the different stages of migration and cultural adaptation and how they can affect immigrants' mental health; the effects of ecological contexts such as racism, discrimination, religious and folk beliefs, and cross-cultural differences in school and work settings on Latino families; cultural patterns of family organization and family life-cycle transitions; and dilemmas which arise for immigrants when confronted with the dominant culture's values in areas such as couple relationships, childrearing expectations, rites of passage, and the role of the elderly in the family. Throughout, Falicov focuses on the issues relevant for mental health treatment. She provides interesting reviews and discussions of the theory and research in each area, discusses helpful treatment approaches, and gives compelling case studies which she minutely deconstructs to illustrate her ideas.

Falicov's approach provides an overarching frame for therapy with multicultural clients irrespective of the therapist's theoretical orientation. Her emphasis is on a humanistic, open, curious stance. She describes her domains as "maps" to guide therapists and borrows techniques from many sources to make the therapy richer and more flexible. The goal of the approach and techniques she suggests is to make clients aware of socioeconomic, political, cultural, and ideological circumstances that constrain their lives as a way to empower them in their personal relationships and in their dealings with their communities and social agencies. For example, a discussion of how the family's social and support network has changed with migration, and the role this may play in their current difficulties, may lead to collaborative problem-solving and an exploration of ways in which the family can take the initiative to recreate some aspects of that network in their new context. Falicov particularly emphasizes certain techniques she has found useful in working with immigrant families, including asking for a "migration narrative" in early sessions, framing certain presenting problems as a process of "cultural transition," and viewing the therapist's role as a "social intermediary" as well as a "family intermediary" at times.

The book includes a very important chapter on racism in all its intercultural and intracultural, societal and familial aspects, and with its myriad implications for immigrants' mental health and for the therapeutic encounter. Falicov tackles a very sensitive subject in an approachable and direct manner while addressing its full complexity. This is a subject which continues to be difficult to explore in any depth, not just with clients, but also in professional conversations amongst colleagues. Her discussion of the often "insidious and unexpected" racism in the therapy encounter is particularly enlightening given the continued pervasive assumptions in the mental health system, such as the assumption that therapist-client ethnic matching is always beneficial. Falicov effectively shows how such an approach frequently lulls therapists into thinking that the therapeutic encounter and the attempted treatment solutions will be free of prejudice, ignoring intracultural racism and intolerance towards a fellow immigrant's preferred adaptations.

Falicov emphasizes the need for therapists to be aware of their own biases and opinions, which are based both on therapists' own multiple contexts and experiences and which significantly affect the therapy process ("perspectivism"). Falicov's weaving of her own story–personal as well as clinical experiences–with her more theoretical writing throughout the book is a very effective tool for fostering such awareness. She sets the example for clinicians to examine in depth their own migration and socialization experiences and how they have dealt with them.

This book poses a challenge for therapists to re-think our positions vis-à-vis cultural issues in our practice and to deal with our own biases and prejudices, however subtle. Falicov "challenges the assumed universality of family therapy theory," reminding us of the many ways in which it belongs to our zeitgeist and may need adjustment before being applied to immigrants from varied cultures. Her ideas are a welcome change from a simplistic view of culture to a more complex one which allows for the full richness of each of our patients to emerge.

Falicov's model serves to organize clinicians' thinking regarding culture and the influence of cultural variables on patients' presenting problems and available solutions, as well as on the therapeutic process. In particular, by thinking in terms of the four domains Falicov proposes, clinicians will encompass a great deal of information and will be less likely to mistake cultural differences for psychopathology or to miss possible issues underlying patients' presenting problems. An advantage of MECA, as compared to ethnographic approaches, is that, due to its exploratory nature, it can be applied when working with any culture with only minimal initial knowledge of that culture's values and beliefs.

Both Falicov's approach and her writing are culturally sensitive, humane, and respectful of differences. Through her case studies, it becomes clear how Falicov avoids stereotyping her patients at every corner and unearths useful information while strengthening the therapeutic alliance. Incorporating her model or some of her suggested techniques into one's teaching and clinical practice will go a long way towards preventing cultural misunderstandings in treatment.

Latino Families in Therapy is a very generous book. Not only does Falicov clearly give of herself by including her own experiences whenever relevant, she also includes information on many techniques developed by other colleagues in the field (such as "cuento therapy"), which clinicians may find useful and can find out more about through her bibliography. With its wealth of rigorously researched information and its clear organization, this book is an ideal resource to go back to and review as often as needed in the training and supervision of clinicians as well as in one's own practice.

In conclusion, this book is a must-read for therapists working with multicultural patient populations. Celia Falicov has imbued culturally sensitive therapeutic practice with a new richness, encouraging therapists to delve into an invaluable therapeutic approach that, for all its complexity, remains straightforward and accessible.

Veronica Barenstein, PhD
Family and Couples Therapy Training Program Coordinator
Psychology Department
Neuropsychiatric Institute
UCLA Medical Center
Los Angeles, CA 90095

GAY AND LESBIAN COUPLES: VOICES FROM LASTING RELATIONSHIPS. By Richard A. Mackey, Bernard A. O'Brien, & Eileen E. Mackey. New York: Greenwood, 1997, 224 pp, $19.95 (paper).

This book continues the previous work done by the same authors on lasting relationships in heterosexual couples (Mackey and O'Brien, 1995). In this book, the authors pick up the tradition initiated by McWhirter and Mattison (1984) in describing gay mens' relationships over the lifespan. As is too often the case in studies of invisible minorities, the sample size was small–72 persons in 36 relationships, including both males and females. To be included in the study, respondents had to be in the same relationship for a minimum of 15 years. It was with this minimum criterion that the authors then looked at the quality of those relationships through the eyes of the participants. The authors include their interview schedule and a description of the open-ended interview process with Ph.D. candidates as the interviewers. Unfortunately, the population studied was potentially biased by the sampling methods (outlined in Appendix A as the "snowball technique"). As a result, the quantitative data (reported in percentages) is probably of much less use than are the qualitative descriptions of respondents' experiences.

Gay and Lesbian Couples is set up to include a significant number of quotations from the respondents as illustrative of the authors' main points. The organizational structure is based on description of roles, relational fit, decision-making, conflict management, intimacy skills (including sexuality), social supports in the larger community, and finally, the book's strongest effort, a summative chapter integrating the authors' findings and ideas.

Strengths of the book include its ability to look at gay and lesbian coupling from a non-heterosexist perspective. Unfortunately, this is still relatively rare in attempts to come to a descriptive understanding of relationships in general, let alone those between gay and lesbian persons. Additionally, the "voices" of the respondents are well represented in the book and, at times, can be interpreted somewhat differently than the authors have done. Nevertheless, the book is easy to read and flows quite comfortably.

However, in reading the book, something appeared to be missing. At first, I thought this was related to the book's almost conversational tone, but later recognized that it had more to do with the significant limitations of the study itself. Unfortunately, 36 couples generated by a potentially biased "snowball" sampling method do not represent the culture at large or even the lesbian and gay sub-culture; the sample of experience described certainly does not convey the modern diverse cultural mosaic. This becomes evident as one continues to read through the book and increasingly experiences an unfortunate but understandable shallowness in its contents. Although topics such as internalized homophobia, financial discrepancy, open and closed sexual intimacies, and family-of-origin issues are addressed in the book, the reader is left feeling rather bereft of diversity in how couples respond to these important issues. One wonders, therefore, if this is mostly related to the poverty in sampling.

Perhaps the book's most interesting conclusion is in the authors' finding that there appear to be no differences in the vast majority of relational values between gay, lesbian and heterosexual relationships. For those of us who know persons in all these relationships, this appears to be an obvious truism, but it may come as a surprise to those who have been struggling with heterosexist and/or homophobic assumptions about gay and lesbian relationships.

In summary, therefore, if one were to put this on a "buy this book" value meter, the meter reading would say: "A loaner from the library."

Gary Sanders, MD
University of Calgary Medical Clinic
Calgary, Alberta
Canada

REFERENCES

Mackey, R.A. and O'Brien, B.A. (1995). Lasting Marriages: Men and women growing together. Westport, CT: Praeger.

McWhirter, D.P. and Mattison, A.M. (1984). The male couple: How relationships develop. Englewood Cliffs, NJ: Prentice-Hall.

WHY HISTORY MATTERS: LIFE AND THOUGHT. By Gerda Lerner. *New York: Oxford University Press, 1997, 249 pp., $13.95 (paperback).*

In this collection of essays Gerda Lerner traces her development as a "feminist thinker and as a historian" from 1980 to 1997. Lerner is best known outside of history circles for her two books *The Creation of Feminist Consciousness* and *The Creation of Patriarchy*. I have been an enthusiastic follower of her work and found this volume of essays to be further enriching. These essays represent a commingling of the intellectual and the personal, of the muses of a scholar and of a woman passionately committed to investigating the sources of her own intellectual quests. From various angles, Lerner explores the implication of her experience as a "Jewish women refugee" with her work as a "scholar concerned with race, class, and gender" (p. xii).

The book is divided into three parts, richly titled "History as Memory (Part I)"; "History: Theory and Practice (Part II)"; and "Revisioning History (Part III)." Rather than examining the chapters sequentially, I feel I can best give a sense of the book's power by showing how Lerner elaborates three or four of the central themes that comprise her major premise that history matters.

Lerner seeks to understand how her status as a Jew and her experience of "otherness" led her to the study of history. She tells us her story–her childhood in Vienna, leaving Austria in 1939, and coping as a new immigrant to the U.S. As she reviews her early memories, delving into the salient details and experiences when she first came to terms with the stark reality of her "otherness," the reader is pulled into an intimately nuanced sense of who she is and how her early perceptions penetrated her. She examines not only how the non-Jewish world viewed her but also how her family of origin reflected upon their own Jewishness and class.

> When we went on summer vacations in the beautiful mountain resorts of Austria, my father impressed us with the need not to 'act Jewish,' that is, we were not to speak with our hands, not to raise our voices, not to be noisy or too lively or too inquisitive. The message again backfired–it told me we were outsiders and ought to hide our deviant, disgraceful status as best we could. (p. 5)

As she ponders her early memories, she is moved to ask how she became an historian? And why, too, had she been an historian who specialized in American women and Black women but who never studied the history of Jewish women? As she intricately threads together childhood memories and her early refugee experience, she concludes, "Experiencing antisemitism and fascism led me to Women's History, for I learned first hand what it means to be defined as 'the Other,' the deviant" (p. 54). She understands how inexorably tied she is to her personal experiences and how they are the driving force of her scholarship. "After the Holocaust, history for me was no longer something outside myself. . . . History had become an obligation" (p. 12).

Lerner enacts her obligation as a teacher of history and builds the supports for her argument inductively by amassing rich resources of historical data. She guides the reader historically through deconstructing the category of race. In the process of learning about how the category of Negro was arbitrarily designated in the 1750s in Virginia, I find myself questioning my own notions and confusions; whether I, as a Jewish woman, am part of a racial group or a religious-ethnic group? Where did this notion that Jews were a distinctive racial group come from? Lerner informs me that Jews were not considered a racial group until Nazism–until then Jews were considered a religious group. The Nazis, like the Virginia plantation owners, arbitrarily designated Jews as a race. Through Lerner we see the eloquent and scholarly development of how "race" is socially constructed. The term "'race" was originally used to mean "kin" and was not biologized until the 19th century. We see how the arbitrary targeting of one group by another based on some visual difference was how conquerors historically designated slaves. Difference has been used historically to justify dominance. "And, historically what makes dominance acceptable is putting a negative mark on difference" (p. 135). Even in the second and third millennia B.C., when visual differences did not exist, they were created by "marking the slaves—with a brand, a particular "way of cutting the hair, a special way of dressing or other means" (p. 134).

Lerner argues against the analysis of race, gender and class as separate categories and demonstrates how they were "inseparable from the start" during the formation of the archaic states (p. 135). She emphasizes, "It is no accident that everywhere the first slaves known are women of foreign tribes" (p. 134). By re-conceptualizing the paradigms of race, class and gender as interacting processes through which hierarchies are maintained, she helps us see how dominance has been constructed throughout history:

> Race, class and gender oppression are inseparable; they construct, reinforce and support one another. The form which class first took historically was generic and racist. The form racism first took was generic and classist. The form the state first took was patriarchal. These are the starting points for re-conceptualization. (p. 143)

Through her careful unfolding of the historical data we see clearly four primary processes through which dominance is constructed. First, there is the process of arbitrary targeting by one group against the other based on some difference. This is followed by a collection of negative characteristics that are arbitrarily selected and attached to the group. Step three is the process by which the discrimination is institutionalized through polices and laws of the state. And finally, step four is marked by the group having a different historical experience from the dominant group's historical story.

What happens to people who have been denied their history, people who have been "denied a usable past" (p. 118). Prior to the documentation of women's history, women and other marginalized peoples and groups were left without a sense of their own history and importance–as if they did not exist and played no part in the development of the world. Lerner believes this kind of invisibility has deleterious psychological impact for peoples' sense of self and their place in society. "The necessity of history is deeply rooted in personal psychic need and in the human striving for community . . . Groups so deprived have suffered a distortion of self perception and a sense of inferiority based on the denigration of communal experience of the group to which they belong" (p. 118).

Through different pathways–the personal and the scholarly–Lerner teaches us how history matters and the essential part it plays for the understanding of self and society. "It is not a dispensable intellectual luxury: history-making is a social necessity" (p. 116). Her personal tone and riveting intellectual rigor makes this collection a rich resource for the feminist family therapist. In her language and in her ideas, she is exquisitely sensitive to the nuances and paradoxes of otherness, marginality and invisibility, domination and collusive subordination, all of which are vividly composed into a richly woven tale of her life and the life of others.

Lois Braverman
Private Practice
Des Moines, IA

9780789011527.